Instead of a Letter

Also by Diana Athill

INSTEAD

OF A

LETTER

— a memoir —

Diana Athill

W. W. Norton & Company • New York • London

First published in the United States by Doubleday 1962
First published in Great Britain by Chatto & Windus 1963
Published in Great Britain by Granta Publications 2001
First published as a Norton paperback 2010

For information about permission to reproduce selections from this book,
write to Permissions, W. W. Norton & Company, Inc.,
500 Fifth Avenue, New York, NY 10110

For information about special discounts for bulk purchases, please contact
W. W. Norton Special Sales at specialsales@wwnorton.com or 800-233-4830

Manufacturing by Courier Westford
Book design by J. Lops
Production manager: Devon Zahn

Library of Congress Cataloging-in-Publication Data

Athill, Diana.
Instead of a letter : a memoir / Diana Athill.
p. cm.
ISBN 978-0-393-33857-7 (pbk.)
1. Athill, Diana. 2. Authors, English—20th century—Biography.
3. Editors—Great Britain—Biography. I. Title.
PR6051.T43Z466 2010
828'.91409—dc22

2010008488

W. W. Norton & Company, Inc.
500 Fifth Avenue, New York, N.Y. 10110
www.wwnorton.com

W. W. Norton & Company Ltd.
Castle House, 75/76 Wells Street, London W1T 3QT

1 2 3 4 5 6 7 8 9 0

To B. R.
With Love

Instead of a Letter

1

M Y MATERNAL GRANDMOTHER died of old age, a long and painful process. Heart and arteries began to show signs of wearing out when she was ninety-two years old, but it was not until two years later that they failed her and precipitated her—still lucid, still herself—into death. By the end, pain and exhaustion had loosened her grip on life so that when she 'recovered' yet again from a heart attack she would whisper, 'Why doesn't God let me die?' but for a long time she was afraid of what was happening to her. She was afraid of death, and she was sorrowful—which was worse—because she had much time in which to ask herself what her life had been for, and often she could not answer.

I was not much with her at that time. Her son and her daughters, who lived near or with her, laboured through it at her side, but her grandchildren were scattered and saw her only when they visited their parents. But once I happened to be there when she was very ill and everyone was more than usually worn out, so I took a night watch. I sat in her cold room (if the windows were shut she felt suffocated), watching the dark hollows of her eyes and the shocking dark hole of her mouth—it was unbearable that Gran, always so completely in control of appearances, should lie with her mouth agape. I listened to the rhythm of her breathing. Sometimes it would stop for a whole minute and the winter night would be absolutely still. In the long silences I prayed to her God, 'Please, please don't let her start breathing again,' and knew that if she died it would not be frightening, that I should feel peace. But each time the harsh, snoring breaths would begin again, hauling her back to another awakening and to more pain and physical humiliation. It was some weeks after that, when she had rallied to the extent of writing an angry letter to the local paper about a new road of which she disapproved, and of ordering a dentist to her bedside to make her a new set of false teeth, that she turned her beautiful speckled eyes towards me one afternoon and said in so many words: 'What have I lived for?'

It was she who should have been able to tell me that. All her life she had been a churchgoing Christian of apparently unshaken faith. But she was on her own then: not suffering, like Doctor Johnson, from fear of the consequences of her sinfulness according to the teachings of that faith, but simply unsupported by it. I said to her what I believed: that she had lived, at the very least, for what her life had been. The long, hard months of dying could eclipse her life, but they did not expunge it. What she had created for us, her family, by loving and being loved, still existed, would continue to exist, and could not have existed without her. 'Do you really think that it has been worth something?' she asked, and I held her hands and told her that I believed it with all my heart. Then I went away, and wondered. For her it might well be the truth. She had created a world for us. Even if I had been the only one of her descendants to have been rooted in that world (and perhaps I was one of the least deeply rooted of them all), something that her love had made would still be alive. But what of a woman who had never had the chance, or had missed the chance, to create something like that? What of myself? That was a question to whistle up an icy wind, and I was out in it. I waited for the shivering to start.

Well, it has not started yet, and I would like to know why. Which is my reason for sitting down to write this.

2

I T IS STRANGE to have loved someone like my grandmother, with whom I came to disagree on almost everything of importance. In anyone but her the values she held seem to me absurd or shocking, yet there she is: the dominant figure in my curiously matriarchal family, her memory warm with love, pleasure, and gratitude.

When she was a girl, one of four handsome daughters of a Master of an Oxford college, she swore that she would never be kissed by any man but the one she would marry, and she never was. She met her husband when he was an undergraduate: a man with frosty blue eyes and a trace of Yorkshire accent ('cassel' for castle, 'larndry' for laundry), who read for the bar but did not practise for long because he inherited his father's estate, which I shall call Beckton. It was not in Yorkshire but in East Anglia, to which his family had moved because his mother was supposed to be delicate and to need a softer climate. She must in fact have been a hardy woman in spite of delicate looks, for she lived to a good age, and if the climate of East Anglia is softer than that of Yorkshire, heaven forbid that I should ever have to winter in the latter.

My grandmother bore her husband four daughters, of whom my mother was the youngest; and at last, when I suspect that a sense of failure was beginning to prey on her, one son. She despised women, or thought that she did. Intelligent herself, happy to send two of her girls to Oxford when it was still uncommon, and proud of any success her female grandchildren might achieve in unwomanly careers, she yet insisted that women's minds were inferior to men's. There was some kind of ambiguity at work here, for although masculine superiority was never questioned, the climate of my grandmother's house was markedly feminine and her daughters' husbands always seemed to be slightly on the fringe of it. On a subject suitable to men—war, politics, a question of local government, the appointment of a clergyman to a living—she would turn to a son-in-law with a formal deference: 'I have been wanting to ask you—ought I to write to the bishop . . . ?' but if she intended to write to the bishop, that was what she would do, whatever the son-in-law said. It was not that the deference was false, but perhaps it was paid to a figure too masculine, too infallible to exist: a pattern of manhood to which the real men in the family failed wholly to conform.

Whether my grandfather conformed to it or not I do not know, for he died when I was six. If he did not, it was through no fault of his wife's. All I know of their relationship is that their two writing-desks in the library at Beckton Manor were so placed that his was near the fire and hers far from it, and that when, after his death, she referred to him it was always as though he were unquestionable in whatever he said or did. The references were infrequent, but they followed a pattern: 'Grandpapa always said . . . ' and so it was; 'Grandpapa would never let the children . . . ' and so they never did;

'Grandpapa was very fond of . . .' and so it was good. That she had adored him was an article of faith in the family, but during her last illness she disconcerted one of her daughters. They were talking of her fear of death. 'I don't understand why you are so afraid,' said her daughter. 'You have always been religious—surely you believe in an afterlife and that you will meet Dad again?' My grandmother, it seems, said nothing. 'But,' I was told, 'she gave me such a *very odd* look, it quite shocked me.' The look may have referred to the afterlife in general, but her daughter had an uncomfortable feeling that it referred to Grandpapa.

What do I know about him? That he had blunt, North Country good looks; that he had discriminating taste in silver and wine and built up a large and excellent library with its emphasis on history; that when he enlarged Beckton Manor, making it U-shaped instead of L-shaped, he set up a kiln to make small bricks matching those of the house, which was built in about 1760, and employed skilled workmen to carve stone to a Georgian design round his new front door and to mould plaster swags to crown the Adams chimneypiece he put in his new drawing-room. A man of taste, but backward-looking. He would give sixpences to his children for learning *Lycidas* before they were eight, wrote in well-managed Johnsonian cadences a thesis on the Serbs (whom he called Servs), and travelled modestly in Italy and Greece, bringing back stone urns for the terrace wall and insisting that his accompanying children put permanganate in the foreign water with which they had to brush their teeth. He was a good farmer. The estate at Beckton is of a thousand acres, some of the land rented out to tenants but much of it attached to the Manor Farm. My grandfather employed a bailiff from Yorkshire, but he took most of the management on himself and did it well.

I cannot recall any word spoken to me by my grandfather. His children's talk of him has always been as unquestioning as his widow's, and sometimes affectionate. He was not quite a tyrant, perhaps, but they convey that he ruled his roost as though by divine right, and I do not think that I would have liked him. Death lent him a sort of holiness for a time. His soul flew out of open sash windows and 'went to Heaven to be with God,' which gave him a share of God's benevolence. After that he did a miracle for me, permitting me to walk unstung through a bed of nettles. Each spring, when we made cowslip balls for my grandmother's birthday, we put the best of them on his grave, an austere grey slab with the words 'Tomorrow to fresh woods and pastures new' carved on it, but the feeling of piety and love which attended this tribute was engendered by the act rather than directed towards the memory of a real man. And the things I owe him—Beckton as a place in which to grow up, books as an indispensable part of life—soon came to seem Gran's dispensation, not his.

She went on being there. After breakfast she would put on an overall and brush the dogs out on the terrace by the steps which led into the library. Wearing thick leather gloves she would garden in her greenhouse, or the rose beds, would cut flowers for the house and would arrange them in the 'flower room,' where the vases were kept and where the dogs slept. She wrote many letters on small sheets of black-edged paper, in writing so like shorthand that only her daughters knew the secret of reading it. She went for a long walk every day and took a strong dose of senna pods every night: fresh air and open bowels were, she considered, all that was necessary for health. Her housekeeping, to which she paid vigilant attention, was simplified by custom. Vegetables, milk, eggs, and butter all came from the estate;

hams were cured, honey was harvested, or jam was made at fixed times, and the groceries were ordered by post every month, from the Civil Service Stores in London. It was a simple, rhythmical life in which she was only concerned with the management, not the execution, but when much later she moved to a smaller house and staff problems combined with the dwindling of a fixed income forced her to do things herself, she knew how to clean, dust, polish silver, and so on much better than the rest of us, who had been doing it for years as a matter of course.

The pleasures of her life were the place itself, which she adored, her family, and reading: her existence should have been a tranquil one. What was it that made anxiety such a distinct thread in it? Never could anyone go away from Beckton without my grandmother's eyes expressing real unhappiness. The journey might be a short one, made for pleasure, but she still felt a clutch of fear. We were not going to eat enough, and what we ate would be unwholesome; we were going to sleep with our windows shut; we were going to catch some infectious disease; a car was going to skid or a train run off the rails. Bad things were likely to happen to people if they went away. I have noticed this attitude in other people whose lives are secure, comfortable, and sheltered by privilege so that one would expect disaster to be far from their minds. I suppose, whether they recognize it or not, it is an acknowledgment of the forces besieging their position. My grandmother had a good knowledge of history and read *The Times* daily: she knew what was happening in the world. Wars and rumours of war; communists abroad and socialists at home; rising taxes and falling respect for tradition. She, a conservative, a gentlewoman, a devout Protestant Christian and an owner of property, was automatically on the defensive against powers outside her control. She did not trust 'outside' and converted her distrust into fear of accident and careless eating. Over and over again I have heard her, or someone like her, say in a voice of real dismay, 'But you can't go on that train, you'll miss lunch!' as though they had become obsessed by the value of food because of some experience of hardship or starvation. In their time measured out not by coffee spoons but by dishes of roast beef, steak-and-kidney puddings, apple pie and cream, they have never once felt or expected to feel a pang of true hunger, so from where does this irrational panic come if it is not a symbol of something else?

My grandmother's anxiety increased as she grew older, because she felt that the right, the natural order of things would be for her to be able to provide for us all on her death, and it was clear that she could not do so; but when I was a child it was less explicit. It was simply darling Gran fussing, and if you teased her about it she smiled back ruefully, half amused by herself, half expressing 'It is all very well for you to laugh, if only you knew.'

My father had a family, but it did not own Beckton. It owned no land at all. My paternal grandfather, a clergyman in comfortable circumstances, shot himself for no good reason while I was still a baby (the coal had not been delivered on time, I believe: he had high blood pressure and would therefore fly into violent rages over small matters). It was as 'good' a family as my mother's and although it had left East Anglia long ago, it had a better claim than hers on our own beloved county, having several tombs and brasses there to prove the existence of rustic Athill knights and one fishmonger at a respectable distance in time. In spite of this my mother felt it to be a family inferior to hers, and somehow, I can no longer remember exactly in what way, conveyed this idea to her children. She always felt that possession by her was nine-tenths of anything's value, even a dog's. A woman who loved animals to the point of absurdity, she rarely admitted charm or breeding in a dog belonging to someone else. 'It's not a bad-looking puppy, I suppose,' she would say, 'but it's going to be leggy'—or, 'One of those hysterical dogs, always ready to make a fuss of strangers.' In the same way, her husband's family bored and irritated her. It was as though when they were first married and conflicting loyalties emerged—with whom, for instance, should they spend Christmas?—she had said like a child 'Bags I my family,' and had got away with it ever since.

Because of Beckton, this was easy to do. A house with twenty bedrooms, standing in a large garden and park with a thousand acres of land round it, can absorb children far more easily than can a neat six-bedroomed house with a two-acre garden, like that of my paternal grandmother, who lived in Devonshire. It was more *sensible* to go to Beckton for the holidays. And if we or any of our cousins had been ill, or our parents were abroad, Beckton Gran could house us with much pleasure and little inconvenience, while Devonshire Grannie, fond though she was of us, would have had to turn her house upside down. Besides, my father was an Army officer with, during all my childhood, the rank of major, and with private means so small that they hardly counted. He lived above his income, modestly and anxiously, from the day he was married, but even by doing that he could not afford to give his wife and children so good a time as they had at Beckton: he would have felt churlish had he prevented their visits. I doubt, indeed, whether he could have done so if he had tried. My mother was strong-willed and he had the disadvantage of being the one *qui aimait*. So although I and my younger brother and sister knew that our official home was where he happened to be working—Woolwich, or when he retired from the Army and took a job in the city, Hertfordshire—our 'real' home, the place to which we 'came home' from other places, was Beckton.

Having bought a small glass bottle made in about 1785, club-shaped, with a delicate spiral rib from neck to base, I was looking at it with affection, enjoying the colour of the glass and the hint of irregularity in the shape. Why, I began to wonder, are objects made in England during that period so much my home territory when it comes to aesthetic pleasure? The products of other centuries and of other countries I have learnt to appreciate, but I cannot remember having to learn to delight in those of the English eighteenth century. Probably, I concluded, it is because so much of my upbringing took place in an eighteenth-century house. It was a thought with gratifying implications. I am glad that I have not inherited money or possessions, and I *would* be glad if I could be sure that I had not inherited any prejudices or attitudes of mind towards other people, but I liked the idea of a child's mind and eye unconsciously trained by graceful shapes, just proportions, and the details of good craftsmanship. It suggested that whatever faults the middling English gentry might have, they would be likely to possess a certain feeling for grace and style: good for us!

Then, unfortunately, I began to remember various objects

bought by my relatives, prized by them and admired by myself before I left home and began to sniff round museums and listen to the opinions of people better educated in such matters than myself. I remembered certain lamps and pieces of china and materials for curtains or chair covers. . . . It was true that we were all familiar with one kind of beauty so that if any of us became interested in aesthetics, that kind, being familiar, would be easy to start with; but it was clearly not true that we had gained from it any ingrained, generally applicable sense of quality or style. If the inhabitants of Beckton had to buy something new and were unable to afford to go to the right place for it (the family's fortunes have been coasting downhill all my life), choice would be conditioned not by knowledge, but by familiarity. The new object would be a pitiful, decadent bastard of the old and we would be cheerfully blind to the difference between patina and French polish, cut glass and moulded, a graceful curve and a clumsy one. Only a few members of my family had, if left to themselves, more natural taste than the people they most pitied and despised: the dwellers in suburbia. (The working classes were allowed a few distinct and even endearing merits: suburbanites—no!)

New purchases were not often made, partly because everything in Beckton Manor was certainly 'good' in the sense of being solid and enduring, partly because, even early in my lifetime, extravagance was condemned. It was still a rich man's house compared to those of the vast majority, but the family did not feel itself a rich family. There was a strict line drawn between necessities and luxuries, and luxuries were suspect.

During my early childhood, necessities included a head gardener with two men under him, two grooms, a chauffeur, a butler and a footman, a cook and a kitchenmaid with a scullery maid to help them, a head housemaid with two under-housemaids, and my grandmother's lady's maid. They included, too, animals for our pleasure and governesses and schools for our instruction. They included books, and a great deal of wholesome food, linen sheets rather than cotton, and three separate rooms for being in at different times of the day, not counting the dining-room, the smoking-room, the front hall, in which, for some reason, my grandmother always had tea, and the nursery. Capital being inviolate, there can, indeed, have been little income left over after the maintenance of all this at what was felt to be its proper level.

Clothes for my mother's generation and then for us were almost all made at home or in the village, except for the obligatory coat and skirt, and riding clothes, for which we went to a good tailor. My mother, happily for me, was the extravagant one of the family. She used to make gleeful and guilty forays to London for clothes, but it was an adventure, not routine. My grandfather had travelled a little (since it was before I can remember, I see it as Making the Grand Tour), but after his death it was unusual for anyone to take a holiday abroad, while to buy curtains for your bedroom simply because you were tired of the old ones was unheard of. If the old ones fell to pieces so that you *had* to replace them, you only considered the cheaper ranges of material (even my mother never considered the *most* expensive), and then—alas for that instinctive taste which, for a moment, I attributed to us. If you liked pink roses you chose pink roses, regardless of how the rest of the room was furnished. Sometimes you would recognize aesthetics to the point of saying 'The blue in the pattern picks up the blue in the carpet,' indicating a tiny blue motif in the design which, if examined closely, could be seen almost to match an equally inconspicuous blue twirl in the carpet's pattern; or sometimes you would speak the words which have sealed the fate of so many British interiors, and of the appearances of so many Englishwomen: 'It is a good colour because *it goes with anything.'*

Yet Beckton Manor was a charming house to be in, and so are almost all the English houses of its kind that I have known. Like its fellows, it had plenty of lovely things in it by chances of inheritance or the good taste of individuals, and it had something else as well. Its inhabitants might not be interested in decoration, but they were interested in nature: to flowers, trees, skies, landscapes and weather they responded with a strong sense of beauty, and without thinking of it they brought into the house as much of nature as they could. The tables loaded with cut flowers, the flowery chintzes, the indifferent water-colours of beloved places expressed the life lived from the house, and they pleased.

As a child, of course, I thought it not only lovely but inevitable: that was what a house should be. Any house which did not have those things in it, and which did not look out over terrace and park to a lake beyond which rose the Lake Covert (landscaped by Capability Brown, we all mistakenly believed), was only a poor attempt at a house. When my mother scolded me for bragging to a friend of the number of bedrooms at Beckton and the two islands in the lake, telling me that one should never show off about good fortune to those with less, she may have improved my manners but she did not diminish my sense of superiority. Even the cold was a matter of pride. Warmth did not rate as a necessity, since it was held to be the opposite of fresh air and therefore unhealthy, so everyone was crippled by chilblains from November to February. 'My sponge is *often* frozen solid in the morning,' I remember boasting to some less hardy, less fortunate child.

How guilty do I feel at having come in on the tail end of such a life and having loved so passionately a place founded on privilege the earning of which had become remote? I do not often refer to it, and when I think about it a figure appears opposite me: that of some faceless friend brought up in a Manchester back street, with a childhood very different from my own stored in his head. At his most charitable, I feel, he would be giving me a quizzical look; and if I were to repeat to him the kind of thing my grandmother, my parents, my other relatives of their generation and even some of my own would say about his accent, his clothes, his attitudes . . . Well, how could I repeat that kind of thing? And if he were a Jew or a Negro, or some other kind of foreigner not of noble birth (for a foreigner can only be guaranteed a gentleman by a title), then what could he feel towards my background less than disgust?

That smug, matter-of-fact assumption of superiority! Many landed families were richer and better bred than mine; nuances which mine recognized but which made no difference to their certainty. Except when it came to lords, whose acquaintance gave them a pleasure verging on the undignified, they were convinced that they were the best kind of people to be (indeed there was something a little fishy about anyone not a lord who was richer or grander than they were). When my grandparents dismissed someone as 'not a gentleman,' their unthinking certainty had the force of a *moral judgment;* while the tinge of apology or defiance that crept into the same judgment when pronounced by my parents' generation was only faint.

This attitude was at the best comic, at the worst repulsive, for with what could that particular family support its certainty of being 'the best'? The abilities of most of its members were respectable but ordinary, their achievements no more than commonplace. None of them was unusually intelligent or energetic and most of them lacked imagination to a remarkable degree. Generous and affectionate they could be, but they hardly ever extended these qualities outside the family circle. Like anyone else they had their charms, their interesting quirks, their endearing or impressive aspects, and their standard of behaviour was, within certain limits, civilized and reliable, but it was not just in matters of taste that they were no better than anyone else: physically, intellectually, and morally they were no more than middling. Yet they despised almost all the rest of the world, excepting people as nearly as possible replicas of themselves, as though their status as English country gentlefolk made them exceptional beings; something of which they fell short even by their own standards, for they were not well enough connected, and Beckton was not a large enough estate, for them to come anywhere near the top of the ladder of snobbery.

What made my family so profoundly self-satisfied? That question has puzzled me more with every year of my life. The satisfaction in itself was not objectionable, since people can only function comfortably if they have it; but its obverse—the disdain or distrust of anyone not of their kind—that was stupid, ugly, and pitiful, and it is a curious sensation to be bound by enduring ties of love and habit to a set of people who so stubbornly displayed it. All that money spent on education, and so little thinking done as a result of it! Reactions still triggered by the sound of a vowel, the cut of a coat, the turn of a phrase. . . . 'He was wearing what I think he would have called a *sports jacket*,' said one of them, only the other day (he would have called it a tweed coat), and that, as far as the wearer of the sports jacket was concerned, was that. Once imbued with such reactions, it is impossible entirely to escape them: I know that until the day I die I shall be unable to avoid *noticing* 'raound' for 'round,' 'invoalve' for 'involve' (on that one an Army officer of my acquaintance used to turn down candidates for a commission), because a built-in mechanism will always click, however much I dislike it, 'placing' everyone I meet as though for a second it was my parents' eyes and ears at work, not mine. But once it has clicked it can very easily be disregarded. The puzzle lies in the choice not to disregard it.

An old man near death once gave my uncle great pleasure by telling him that a treasured memory—something which had remained for years in his mind as a vignette of the England he loved—had been a glimpse, once caught as he was driving by, of my uncle riding in the park at Beckton. It is a pretty park, well planted with groups of beech and oak trees, sloping gracefully down to the lake beyond which the wood known as the Lake Covert rises, and mildly dominated by the house (to the left of the picture as the old man approached it), standing on its balustraded terrace with a great cedar tree at one corner of it to break its slightly austere Georgian lines. 'It was a perfect October afternoon,' said the old man. 'There was the Lake Covert, all golden in its autumn leaves, reflected in the water, and there were you, cantering along beside the lake on that black of yours—what a beautiful horse he was—

with a couple of dogs running behind you. I watched you and I thought, Now that's a lovely scene, that's England, and I've never forgotten it.'

Describing the conversation, and the old man's emotion, my uncle gave a slight deprecating laugh, but he was not only touched, he was satisfied. That man had recognized in him and his setting what he himself felt deeply to be their true nature, and as he savoured it he was likable rather than absurd. He was moved by a vision of something which he dearly loved and which had comforted him when, during the war, he was badly wounded: he felt genuinely that it was worth dying for. To have said to him, 'But you are not England. You and what you represent are only a tiny fraction of England and an archaic one at that, preserved not by deeds or virtue but by money most of which you yourself do not earn'—to have said that would have been to have attacked not a fancy but a rooted belief. He might have answered, 'All right, so it is preserved by money: money in the hands of the right people, of people like us. What further argument do you need for the existence of such people and such money?' He and his like have been snug all their lives, and snugness breeds smugness—but smugness is too small a word for what it feels like *from inside.* From inside, it feels like moral and aesthetic *rightness;* from inside, it is people like me, who question it, who look stupid, ugly, and pitiful—and ungrateful, too. Why admit that the grammar-school boy, the self-made businessman, the artist, the foreigner or whatever are just as likely to be 'the best' as we are, when such an admission must attack certainty, the cosiest of all the gifts bestowed by privilege? It is not only ingratitude, it is treachery.

Treacherous I may be, but ungrateful I am not. I consider it good fortune to have been born of Beckton's youngest daughter, not of its son, at a point in time and a position in the family where diminishing resources had brought unthinking certainty up against the facts of life and worn it comparatively thin. Never to have broken through its smothering folds would have been, I have always thought, extremely depressing. But on the other hand, not to have enjoyed a childhood wrapped warmly in those folds—that would be a sad loss. There I used to be, as snug and as smug as anyone, believing with the best that we were the best—and if security is the thing for children, which it surely is, then how lucky I was.

Beckton and Gran: they blur together. When I think of her I may see a handsome woman with crisp, pure-white hair (it turned when she was thirty), wearing a black, black-and-white, or grey dress with a cross-over bodice and a lace collar (she was in her eighties before she forgot her widow's status to the point of wearing a dress made of soft, pinky-red wool). Her eyes, with lids that droop slightly in an odd way at the outer corners, are speckled green and grey, capable of an ironic expression but usually full of affection, and she will be looking at me attentively, ready to be amused or interested by what I am saying (for one did not say to Gran the things which would have shocked or displeased her). I may see this woman, or I may think of getting out of the car to open the white gate between park and lawn, breathing that first, almost drinkable, smell of grass, flowers, and cedar tree which was the assurance that we were home. Then images come crowding in: the stream in the kitchen garden in which the newts and tadpoles lived; the marble children under a tree on the library chimneypiece; the scalloped black-green leather which would pull off from the edges of the nursery bookshelves; the goat-shed in the lower stable yard made into a bower of beech branches by a cousin and myself, because tender young beech leaves on the branch were what our goats liked best (we gave them senna pods, too, when we thought they needed them, and sometimes an aspirin or a spoonful of cough linctus). Very clear is the chasm between the back of the sofa and the bookshelves in the morning room, where I would squat for hours to read bound volumes of *Punch,* and the smell of the plush curtains over the double door between morning room and front hall, in which I had only to muffle myself, at one time, in order to begin writing a play in which a cousin was to take the part of a good, blond and slightly insipid princess while I was to be the dark, wicked one, like Sir Rider Haggard's She-Who-Must-Be-Obeyed. 'Go and play in the morning room, darlings,' people would say. It was the room to which children graduated from the nursery, where one could bounce on the furniture or litter the floor with Meccano or cutting-out.

There was only one unpleasant thing in that house: the ghost in the night nursery, where at our smallest we usually had to sleep. It was not an ordinary ghost but a disgusting presence, a slimy grey thing like a stubby elephant's trunk which reached down over the gutter and groped at the window one morning while I was sitting alone on my pot. No one liked that room, which was at the back of the house, looking out on to a gloomy thicket of yew trees, on the old principle, not otherwise observed, of pushing children out of the way with the servants. But no one thought of telling my grandmother about that, so it was nothing to do with her. Every other sound, smell, and texture in the place I loved quite consciously from the earliest time I can remember, and I loved it so much not only because I felt it to be beautiful, but because its presiding genius, my grandmother, loved me.

In relationships outside her family she was not a loving woman, nor a tolerant one. Her servants she distrusted, not (the older, long-established ones anyway) in terms of honesty so much as of sense. She expected them to be ninnies, and to be dirty, and how they managed not to be the latter is hard to see, considering that it was years before anyone thought of putting in a bathroom on the attic floor where they lived, while they were not allowed to use ours. Of people who differed from her on politics or religion she was fiercely scornful, particularly of anyone who believed that the Pope spoke God's word, or who was a socialist. Of foreigners she was not only scornful, but distrustful as well. If they thought that they could govern their own countries better than we could she considered them both fools and traitors. Outside the ramifications of what might be called the greater family as opposed to the central family—the second cousins and so on, about whose fortunes she was always completely and mysteriously informed and whom she wished well—she had no intimate friends.

Described like this, she sounds a disagreeable woman, yet no one ever met her without being charmed. The charm came from the warmth of her personality, and the warmth came from the dynamo of love at work in her for the benefit of her children and her children's children. She was not soft with them. She mocked them if their politics veered to the left, scolded them if they did not eat properly, and criticized any folly they might get up to unless it was something really grave, like marrying a foreigner or having an extra-marital love affair. About that kind of thing she would either keep silent, or would choose not to know. But although her family could cause her impatience or grief, they could not diminish her love—and the only grief they could have caused her when still young would have been by illness or death. In her house we could be excited by our own misdemeanours, but we could never feel that they put us in peril, so for us this autocratic woman, whose sharp intelligence was deliberately confined to so narrow a range, created a benign air which we could always breathe again, even in middle age, simply by going back to the place where she lived.

I shocked her once. I was about ten years old and had thought of an image for life. I thought that it was as though people were confined in a bowl which was floating on a sea. While snug at the bottom of the bowl they lived their lives complacently, but the bowl spun and tossed on the sea and its spinning sometimes sent one of them up its side until he could see over the rim. All round would be the endless chaos of dangerous, cold grey water, unsuspected till then, and anyone who had seen it and had understood that what he had thought was safety was only a little bowl, would not be able to bear it. That, I decided, was the origin of madness. I was proud of this idea, described it to my grandmother, and was disconcerted to see her so upset. It was not at all clever, she said sharply, to think that life was aimless, and she told me to remember the then Prince of Wales, who had recently made some statement of high purpose and idealism to a gathering of Boy Scouts.

I was disappointed by this response, which did not seem to me to recognize the implications of my idea, but I remember it because in spite of my disappointment, its inadequacy did not matter. I noted that in some ways I would have to differ from Gran but I did not feel betrayed, because there she was as she spoke, wearing the kind of dress she always wore, with her beautiful hair and her dear, kind eyes watching me with the anxiety I thought was a joke and the love which I would never think of questioning. I myself might incline more to the bowl theory than the Prince of Wales theory, but clearly whatever Gran believed was *good*, because it was believed by Gran.

3

FELT OUTRAGED WHEN someone first pointed out to me that my grandmother's house was not 'mine.' When she died, or decided to make way for my uncle, it would be his, and then his son's, or, if he had no son, his daughter's. Supposing he had no children, I asked hopefully (he was still unmarried at the time). Working on the assumption that succession to the estate would follow the pattern established by the monarchy, it appeared that at least twelve people, seven of them my contemporaries, would have to die before I would have a claim, and I hardly felt I ought to pray for this however much I would have liked to.

Perhaps this realization came near the time when I lay sprawled on short grass in the back park one spring morning—there were lambs about, and daisies—facing the knowledge that in three years' time I would be thirteen. What made the passage of so long a stretch of time real to me I cannot remember, but it was appalling, giving me a horrible sensation as though my insides had gone cold and empty. To be in my teens, I saw suddenly, would be to leave childhood behind, to be in a world where impossible things could happen. I would become able to believe that the place would go to my uncle; I would become able to foresee a time when, perhaps, I could no longer return to it as though it were my home. Where would my home be? Some place like those in which I had already lived with my parents and brother and sister; a house and garden just big enough for us, with none of our past worked into it and no territory round it to call our own. Already, when we rode across country from the house my parents rented in Hertfordshire, we had to *ask permission* from the owners of the land, which had seemed to me humiliating. And the business of earning my living—it would not be something my father talked about when he was feeling pompous ('You will have to earn your living one day'), but something I should have *to do*. I do not think that I was shocked by the prospect; only frightened. It would surely be difficult and disagreeable, and, because the norm of existence was life at Beckton, it would be unnatural.

In fact, my grandmother went on living in the house until the beginning of the war, when I was twenty-two; it was fully there to go back to. But whoever had given me that early, painful glimpse of the truth had done me a good turn. From that time my love of Beckton began, slowly, to take a wistful, nostalgic turn: I felt that I must treasure every detail of it against the future, and I remember standing under the great beech tree by the lawn, trying to will some essence of myself into the still green air so that after I was dead my ghost would materialize there. But at the same time my fear of what would follow began, with acceptance of mutability, to rub away and other things entering my life increased in value. That

particular bowl, it seemed, spun on no grey sea. It would be sad to
be pushed over the rim, but what surrounded it was a landscape,
and the landscape, as it became increasingly real, began to look
interesting.

My fear of 'thirteen' had been prophetic, all the same, for I believe
I had reached that age when my mother told me that we had 'lost
our money.' What really happened was that, having lived above
their income for too long, my parents were at last rapped over
the knuckles by their bank. We were in the Hertfordshire house
at the time, my father having retired from the Army to avoid
transporting his reluctant family to India, and taken a job in the
City with a firm connected with the mining of mica. Our house
was called The Cottage, but it had six bedrooms and was staffed
with Margaret, the cook; Violet, her sister, who was not exactly a
nanny but looked after the children; Ursula, the governess; Doris,
the housemaid; Mrs Knight, who 'came in,' and deaf Gatwood,
full-time gardener. My parents felt that they were living austerely
because we ourselves looked after our ponies and they had not kept
on their own hunters, nor did they indulge in any luxuries. My
mother had no fur coat and no jewels except a couple of mediocre
diamond rings and the string of small pearls given her as a wedding present by her father. There was rarely any drink in the house
beyond a bottle of sherry, and the furniture was a job lot of stuff,
none of it valuable or beautiful and some of it as utilitarian as the
hospital beds inherited from a convalescent home for officers run
by a great-aunt during the 1914–18 war. According to their lights,

my father and mother were not extravagant people, but still the bank said that unless they followed a certain clearly defined plan they might not cash any more cheques.

My mother did not take this with any enduring seriousness, being a practical and energetic woman with no objection to doing things for herself, and having the comfortable feeling that Beckton was still there in the background. She broke the news to me, however, with an almost dramatic gravity—she always had an appetite for 'the worst'—so that I was impressed.

'Are we really *poor?*' I asked.

'Yes, darling, I'm afraid so.'

'Will Violet have to go? And Ursie?'

'Yes, I expect you will go to school.'

Doris, Margaret, and Mrs Knight went too, and we had to make our own beds and dust the bedrooms. As my mother said soon afterwards, 'the really *bloody* thing about being poor is that if you leave something on the floor when you go out, you know that it *will still be there* when you get back.' At that time I was exchanging two letters a term with a boy I had been in love with since I was nine years old, and I must have described our plight because I remember a letter of his beginning, 'Dear Diana, I am sorry to hear that you are now poor.' I was touched by his delicacy in saying no more about it than that.

It was not long before Beckton came to the rescue. We were going to leave Hertfordshire and live at the Manor Farm, we were told, and to the children the whole thing instantly became a delight. My mother probably had other reasons for making the move, but to us it seemed merely the happy solution of the family's financial problems, and we were so pleased by it that it did not occur to us to worry about my father, who would continue to work in London and could not, therefore, live so far from it except at week-ends. He took lodgings with the family of a man who had once been his own father's coachman, and bicycled to the station every day because my mother had to have the car. I suppose that we felt, vaguely, that it was horrid for him, but it was a relief not to have him in the house. My brother and I had worked out a formula by then: 'Mummy and Daddy are both very nice people, but they don't suit each other, they should never have got married'—this, perhaps, was borrowed from Ursula or Violet. They were quarrelling fiercely at the time, and it was a relief not to have to watch for signs of trouble and to know that if, at weekends, it came (as it usually did) it could only last for two days.

I always *liked* my father—he was a likeable man—but if I ever felt anything warmer than liking it was when I was so young that I cannot remember it. I did not consciously take my mother's side when they quarrelled (indeed, I often felt something like hatred for her irrational flares of temper, and considered that my father, not she, was in the right)—but in our nerves all three of us children were more sympathetic to her than we were to him. It was not until much later that I understood the trouble to come from the simple but deadly poison of physical incompatibility which my father did not feel and my mother had been too inexperienced to recognize during their courtship, but even as small children we could sense the nature of her irritability.

To be constantly loved and desired by someone whose touch is repulsive to you is a profound outrage. You may be in such a situation by your own fault or folly, but whatever the surface facts, you remain the situation's victim because the offence you are receiving goes beyond reason, into such deep recesses of your being. Feeling wicked for her reactions, my mother stubbornly and bravely, though with occasional half-rebellions, went on being my father's wife, but her offended nature got its own back in many ways, and her children's instincts chimed with her instincts more readily than they did with my father's reason.

The scenes were always over trivialities. My mother was an impatient person, hating to wait about, hating slow meals, hating almost to hysteria being late for anything. My father was slow, deliberate, unpunctual. Taking his time over anything gave him a positive pleasure—as it does me. If, on a shopping expedition, he went into the post office to post a registered letter, he would certainly find someone with whom to gossip. Waiting with us in the car, my mother would know that he would do this: she would begin to simmer before two minutes were up. I would resent the way she was working up for a scene, since time mattered to me as little as it did to my father, but still I would begin to feel irritated by his slowness, even to despise it. My brother and I, in the back of the car, would exchange warning looks, and later one of us might say, 'Why is Daddy so *silly*—he always does just the thing to make her lose her temper.' Another thing in which, by nature, I was on my father's side but which came to irritate me, was his scrupulous honesty. He was the sort of man who will seek out the guard on a train to pay the excess fare if a crowd has caused him to travel in a first-class compartment with a second-class ticket. My mother had a streak of bandit in her, was usually prepared to get away with what she could, and used deliberately to enrage him by describing some minor delinquency of her own. With one side of me I admired my honourable father, but with another I saw him as absurd. Because my mother's irritation with him on such matters was a symptom, a release of nervous tension through permissible outlets, it had an infectious force beyond its apparent triviality.

Apart from this, my father did not much care for children. He was always pleasant to us, but he did not find childishness in itself seductive. When he sang, 'Bat, bat, come under my hat, and I'll give you a slice of *ba-a-a-a-con*,' or 'Bony was a warrior,' he was funny and we enjoyed it. We thought him clever when he made up nonsense verses for us, and later wrote plays for us to act, but the things he enjoyed doing with us were things which he enjoyed doing anyway because they exercised his talents or his sense of humour. Just to be with children, to watch them, to enter into their imaginations, was no pleasure to him, and he had no physical rapport with them. Nowadays I sometimes watch my brother handling three small sons, and I see exactly what it was that my father could not feel. My brother will throw his boys about, fondle them, sniff them, stand by a window to watch them as they play in the garden with an unconscious smile of pure pleasure on his face. He loves them with a comfortable, animal warmth, and they respond to it like crocuses in the sun. That is something that was outside my father's nature.

Much of myself comes from my father—my equable temperament, my powers of detachment, my enjoyment of poetry and of the absurd—and the better I knew him as an adult, the more clearly I saw that he was an agreeable, intelligent, upright and witty man. But I never felt closely bound to him; never felt, as I did about my mother, that for good or ill, this person and myself were made of the same substance.

So being separated from my father for so much of the time seemed, when I was thirteen, more of an advantage than otherwise, while living at the Farm—*that* was delight. It was a house to which we could go only to be happy. We knew it intimately, having already stayed there when we were younger and my father was abroad, and spending much of our time there when we were at the Manor. My mother's generation had passed legendary holidays there, to be near my great-grandparents. It was part of Beckton and for children the best part: a pleasure ground richer and more absorbing than garden or park, with the real business of the country going on in it. The first time we had stayed there, my brother and I had become distressed in our loyalties, because surely it was impossible for us to love any place better than Gran's house, and yet . . . It was my brother, then six years old, who had discovered the pleasures of nostalgia for us. We shared a large bedroom looking out over the farm-yard, at the end of a passage and remote from the rest of the family so that we could talk and play with impunity for what seemed like hours after we had gone to bed. One evening, when we were leaning out of the window watching the horses drinking after late haymaking, a cuckoo began to call in the distance. 'Listen,' said my brother. 'It makes me feel funny—it makes me think terribly of being at the Manor.' I listened, and soon each hollow note seemed to be struck on my own heartstrings: tears began to come into my eyes. Past summers—not just the eight I had lived, but innumerable past summers, long and golden, and all experienced at Beckton Manor, seemed to be saying goodbye.

A few days later we discovered that when we heard a cuckoo while at the Manor, we could summon up exactly the same feeling for the Farm. After that we decided that the two houses were part of the same place, so that it did not matter which we loved best.

They were less than half a mile apart. You went out of the back door of the Manor, into the gravelled space between its two wings which in summer was decorated with tubs of fuchsias, down past the stables, through the bottom orchard and a corner of the plantation girdling the kitchen garden, and past three beech trees on which everyone had, at one time or another, carved their initials. The highest initials had grown blistered and blurred; the lowest—mine and my brother's—were clear and still the colour of sawdust. From there a footpath ran along the bottom of the back park beside a line of bat willows planted by my great-grandfather (they were never made into cricket bats, reaching and passing their prime during the last war, when no cricket bats were being made). This led to the stream, at the point where it slid over a little weir to become the beginnings of the lake. You crossed it on a broad footbridge, pausing to drop sticks into the water or just to stare into it, and came to the water meadow—a boggy meadow crisscrossed with little ditches choked with marsh marigolds and ragged robin. The path here was slightly raised, with planks, usually collapsed, over the drains which traversed it. We knew it so well that even in darkness we could tell where we had to take a long stride, or step to the left, or balance carefully because a plank was extra narrow. At the far side of the water meadow the path rose steeply to the small wooden gate into the Farm orchard, and at the top of that was the benevolent Dutch end-gable of the house, curving comfortably above white walls and partly screened by the row of beeches which bordered the back yard. The working buildings sprawled to the left, not at that time the responsibility of those who lived in the house, but definitely part of their territory. This house was to be the background of my growing up (we continued to live there, all but rent-free, for about twelve years); but the love we all felt for it was already established and was rooted in the knowledge we had of it from our earliest childhood.

Mouse droppings, husks of oats quivering in spiders' webs, piles of old sacks—the musty smell of a loft would make me hesitate now. I would stoop to avoid the wispy grey shreds hanging from rafters which cling to one's hair, step carefully to avoid the fangs of disused machinery. But when we were children we shinned along beams over which old pieces of stiff, cracked harness had been looped, and jumped off them into the hay at the end of the loft, near the chute down which it slid to the stable, raising a cloud of dust as we landed, so that motes swam for minutes on end. ('Never jump down into hay: there might be a chopper or a pitch-fork buried in it. A little boy once jumped into a pile of hay and was cut *right in half.*') The picture of the farm buildings I carry in my mind is framed by the loft window—the opening into space with a pulley above it up to which sacks were hauled. When we were small my brother and I would squat there as silent as cats, unobserved, watching the cowman cross the yard with buckets of skimmed milk for the calves, or a horseman bringing in a pair of butterball-smooth Suffolk Punches, unharnessing them, then sending them with a slap on the rump to drink endlessly from the tank, burying their nostrils in the scummy water, after which they liked to hang about in the yard taking their ease for a while, until the man shouted at them and they plodded into the stable, each to his own place. They had names like Tory, Prince, Captain, Bess. When Tory died a new Tory took his place, but he had a different character, he should have had another name.

The granary had a dusty smell, too, but not like the loft's. Wheat, oats, barley, and sometimes beans—they were heaped like sand dunes and each made a different sound when you thrust your hands into the heap, or waded in it—which was forbidden because it scattered the grain. The stables, the cowsheds, the various yards in which animals were kept at different stages of their lives, all of them had their own smells, and none of the smells, however dungy, seemed to us displeasing. An adult watching children scurrying about a farm must see their movements as mysterious, like those of animals. What makes them decide to sit on a certain wall, stare solemnly for perhaps ten minutes at a certain pig, then jump down and run into a barn, clamber to the top of a pile of sugar beet? It is like the flitting of birds from tree to hedge. But I can remember that each building, each activity, each time of day had its own value and meaning—we went from one to another as an adult would decide to drop in at a picture gallery, or go into a shop to buy bread.

'Going to look at the bull,' for example, was not a random whim but an accepted pastime. A bull is a spectacle in himself. We hoisted ourselves up the stout timbers of his loose-box, and with our elbows on the top of the partition would stare at him while he stared back. Placid he might be (and our bulls usually were), but not to be trusted, they said: a bulk of violence rested behind that curly forehead and those small eyes, and when he shifted his feet in the straw or blew through his nostrils there was a shadow of threat in it. If, while we were watching him, the bull piddled or let his red penis protrude from its sheath, we counted it an event. He was sex as well as violence, and we were in awe of him.

The men who worked on the farm were patient and kind. The cowmen were too busy to be interesting companions, but the horsemen had time to talk as they took their teams out to the fields, and would let us ride with them either on a broad back or on a loaded wagon (how it would heave and rock, and sometimes the branches of a tree would sweep it so that you had to flatten yourself on the load). The man whose company we most enjoyed was the shepherd. He was alone a lot in outlying pastures, living out in a hut on wheels during the lambing season, and he was glad to talk. He presided over the most interesting ceremonies of the year: lambing, dipping, and shearing. His dogs were watchful and aloof to anything but their master and their job, so that if they wagged their tails when one spoke to them, one felt flattered. Like all shepherds, ours knew his sheep as individuals, and this seemed a magic power.

For a time, when I was about eight, the shepherd had a boy working with him called Jack Grey. Perhaps he was fifteen years old, but to my brother and me he seemed almost grownup. His father, who was the woodman, came of gypsy stock and Jack had gypsy talents: he could make sounds which rabbits mistook for other rabbits, he poached, he could climb any tree and knew everything about birds and animals. We envied and admired him for living out of doors so much, and at the same time were impressed by his matter-of-fact attitude towards it, his remarks implying that we would not enjoy it as much as we supposed if it were part of a job. We collected birds' eggs then, under strict injunctions to take nothing unless there were at least four eggs in the nest and never to frighten the parent birds so that they would desert. Jack could climb higher trees than we could and was uninhibited by rules (which were awkward in the cases of birds which laid only two or three eggs). The treasures of our collection—our jay's, our heron's, and our sparrow hawk's eggs—came from him. We were with him whenever we could be, and he treated us as equals, not as children. Later he shot at and wounded his father, who had come home drunk and had threatened him. He pleaded self-defence but was sent to prison. Much later, when I was eighteen or nineteen, I was at a roller-skating rink (roller-skating had become a passion with me and my friends) and the attendant, a man at once sleek and seedy with heavily oiled hair and a flashy checked suit, knelt down in front of me to fasten my skates. He did not look up. I looked down at the hair plastered in straplike segments across the bent head, and I heard my voice—this is quite literal, I was unconscious of recognition or of forming words—I heard my voice saying 'Jack Grey.' He looked up and said 'Hullo, Miss Dinah,' and then, after 'How are you' and 'It's a long time,' we were at a loss. The exact nature of our earlier intimacy, what we had talked about besides birds and animals, I could not remember, but I was sharply aware of the ghost of friendship standing there between me and this shady-looking man. We smiled at each other shyly and I left the rink feeling shaky and unhappy. Perhaps as a boy Jack had welcomed the company of small children so kindly because already there were things in his life of which he needed to avoid thinking. I hope he knew how much we loved and admired him.

The friendships children make with their family's employees

seem to the children friendships between equals. If a cowman, or my grandmother's head gardener, caught us at some mischief and said 'I'll tell your grandma on you,' the words were, to us, no more than a formula: it was not the threat but the wrath of the speaker which had authority. It never occurred to us that even when the gardener caught us stealing his beloved grapes he would never actually clout us, nor did we notice that however intimate we were with Jack Grey, he never invited us to his house, nor we him to ours. A relationship which felt natural was possible because the lines laid down for it were so deeply engraved by time and custom that neither side thought of questioning them, but those lines defined a narrow area. When we went back to the Farm 'for good' I was in my early teens, no longer a child. I knew all the men on the farm, of course, but without realizing it I had moved out of the realm of friendship with them.

We were still at our poorest for our first year or so at the Farm, still without servants, though a woman used to come in to do the scrubbing and another to cook lunch. Soon after we settled in, I was sent to the back yard to bring in the cold meat we were going to eat for supper. It was kept in a perforated tin meat-safe hung on the wall in a cool place. I opened the safe, took out the dish—and the shelf was bare. For the first time since my mother had told me about our poverty I felt afraid: *there was nothing in our larder once that meat was eaten.* At the Manor the larder was an L-shaped room with a brick floor and wide shelves made of slate on which were crocks of preserved eggs, flat pans of milk waiting to have the cream skimmed off them, tins and tins of cakes, biscuits and buns, joints of meat, at least one ham, strings of sausages, pounds of butter, big cheeses, bowls of dripping, bottles of fruit, stone jars of currants—food on which the house could have lived for days if it had suddenly been cut off from the outside world. Whatever the breakfast dish in that house—kidneys on toast, or kedgeree, or bacon and mushrooms—there was always an egg boiled for every person there. A houseful of us could amount to sixteen or so, and sometimes no one ate a boiled egg (what *did* happen to them?). At our house in Hertfordshire the scale had not been so grand, but always beside what we were then eating there had been the remains of what we had eaten recently and something that we were soon going to eat: the larder had continuity. I stood in front of the empty meat-safe telling myself that it was silly to be scared, my mother would be buying more food tomorrow, but for a few moments poverty had become real. And because food did reappear on the shelf (and as soon as my mother had recovered her nerve, accumulated there as merrily as ever), I soon concluded that ours was not real poverty. I remained far away from the real thing, I hardly ever had the chance of glimpsing it, but that moment in the back yard had made me feel what a bare shelf was like, and understand that it could happen. It would be an exaggeration to say that it made me think, but it may have given me the beginnings of a sense of proportion.

My mother resembled my grandmother in her generosity towards her children. I never heard her say it, but she must have resolved that we, at least, should not suffer from the financial muddle into which the family had drifted, and it is only now that I see how much unfamiliar work she did about her house at that time. All she expected from me (my sister was five years younger) was that I should help her make beds and clean the bedrooms in the morning, wash up supper and sometimes cook it. It was almost always eggs, usually scrambled—she did not know any other cooking to teach me. Housekeeping generally became rough and ready—a pleasant state for children—and although even at that it must have weighed on her, it was never a bogy for anyone else. She did not mind things which ought to shine not shining, and she did not mind 'clean' dirt (earth, grass seeds, spilt dog biscuit). While there was a carelessly arranged vase of flowers on every surface flat enough to hold a vase, she felt her drawing-room pretty, and so it was. It smelt lovely, too, more like a garden than a room, and since most of its untidiness came from the litter of books on chair arms, foot-stools, and occasional tables, it was an agreeable room to be in.

That accumulation of books silting up the flower-free surfaces in the house: that, at bottom, I owe to my grandfathers. Both were men who took it for granted that a gentleman should have a good library, and my maternal grandfather's library was a very good one. In addition to this, my grandmother's father had been Master of an Oxford college, which meant that however unscholarly his descendants might be, they all esteemed scholarship: they might not read much (most of them, in fact, did), but they considered a house without books in it uncivilized. At the Manor, not only was the library walled with books, but the morning room and my grandfather's smoking-room as well, while the whole of one upstairs passage was given over to shelves containing more trivial volumes (delightful shelves, badly lit, from which you might fish a handbook on veterinary surgery or *The Scarlet Pimpernel*). There was an angle of bookshelves ceiling-high in the nursery, and although reading in the bath, in the w.c., or in bed was forbidden to the younger children, everyone knew why one did it.

Reading ran in two currents. My grandfather's interest had been history, and most of the family, including my mother, inherited his tastes. Gibbon's *Decline and Fall of the Roman Empire* was my mother's bedside reading for a long time, and she knew Horace Walpole, Madame de Sévigné, and Mrs Delaney like old friends. On the other hand, one particularly beloved aunt, and my father, most enjoyed imaginative writing and poetry. My mother had no patience with books which were 'not true.' She always insisted that she actively detested poetry, finding it a lot of words about nothing, and she would not go to see a play by Shakespeare. My father revelled in Shakespeare and made frequent sorties into one poet or another. During the second world war, when, to his great content, he was back in the Army and serving abroad, he suddenly decided that he must read Dryden and wrote home for his complete works.

In a life where the adults took books so much for granted, it was natural that the children should do so too. About eighty per cent of our birthday and Christmas presents always consisted of books: it would have been impossible not to have become a compulsive reader. I developed the lust early and violently, following my father's tastes rather than my mother's, and would smuggle an electric torch to bed almost as early as I can remember so that I could continue to gobble my books under a tent of sheets. I was always puzzled by how *they* knew. Thump, thump, the steps would come along the passage, under the pillow would go book and torch and I would screw my eyes shut, but the minute the light went on and 'they' saw my body stretched so rigidly innocent under the blankets, they would say accusingly, 'You were reading!'

At other times they would say 'You must be skipping,' or 'You can't remember books if you read so many at a time, so fast,' but I never skipped, and any that I understood I did remember. Failing to understand did not prevent my reading. Before I was twelve I had been through most of Meredith in my grandfather's handsome, vellum-bound edition, undeterred by the fact that the involved prose was too much for me. Those submerged, and it was only years later, when I picked up *The Egotist* for what I thought to be the first time, that I rediscovered those sessions on the window seat in the morning-room. Pages of it seemed new to me, then I would come to a 'visual' passage—Clara wearing pink ribbons, finding her young man asleep under the cherry tree, for instance— and I would think, But I have been here before, I have *seen* this, and gradually the whole thing swam up: the slight warmth of the radiator boxed in under the window seat, the green damask on the flat cushion, the smooth binding and the thick, handmade paper with its ragged edges, and my grandmother coming in and saying 'Darling, are you really *enjoying* all those Merediths? He's rather grown-up for you.'

Boys, poor creatures, became part-exiles from our world when they were about eight years old and were sent to their preparatory schools. Girls stayed at home, with governesses. I had run through seven of them by the time we settled at the Farm, starting with 'nursery governesses' whom I shared with my brother (two years younger than myself), and going on, when he had been exiled, to better-qualified women shared with cousins or the daughters of neighbours. With ponies, goats, dogs, streams, tree houses, fruit stealing, and poetry writing to compete against, lessons could hardly be anything but a chore, and I suppose that it is this which has left me with an ineradicable feeling that work is the opposite of pleasure. I have tried to persuade myself out of this, but in vain. After twenty years of working in jobs usually congenial, I still leave my office with the sensation of returning to life.

One of the governesses was sacked because she cowed us, to be forgotten quickly and thankfully. The rest were forgotten slowly and naturally, simply because they meant little to us. Fragments of them remain. A very early one had a kind horse face and was a sucker. Once, when I had irritated her beyond endurance and she had gone out of the room to recover her temper, I leant out of the window, picked a fat, creamy-pink rose from the wall, and laid it on her open book. My eyes must surely have been beady with calculation when she came back to the table, but she noticed nothing, she fell for it, her silly heart melted at the charming ways of children, and I felt a delicious sense of power.

More of Mademoiselle remains because we were cruel to her, and we had not until then realized that it was possible for children to be cruel to grown-ups. Her poor hands purple with chilblains, she would sit there weakly accepting our assurance that it was the custom in England to eat boiled eggs with honey, mustard, Ovaltine, and a pinch of birdseed stirred into them (we did it for several mornings to prove our point). Then she turned, and forced my sister, the baby of the family and not strictly under her jurisdiction, to eat all the fat on her cutlet. My brother and I did not think much of my sister at the time, but she rose to the occasion so well, being instantly sick on the table, that we rallied to her with cries of 'Poor little girl, you have been *cruel* to her,' and bolted into shrubberies and beyond, where we stayed all day, knowing that Mademoiselle would not venture further than lawns and flower gardens. We came in that evening knowing that we had been very naughty, but our mother used other words. 'You have been unkind,' she said. 'How could you have been so cruel to poor Mademoiselle?' The incident engraved a trace of uneasiness on my conscience which made me slightly less horrible than some to the duller, plainer mistresses once I was at school.

Only one governess remains solidly a person: Ursula, the last of them, who stayed with us for five years. Her broad red face and her thin, cottony hair augured ill for her, but her common sense and her affectionate heart soon prevailed. She loved dogs, she could corner a recalcitrant pony in a paddock almost as efficiently as my mother, she made jokes we thought funny, and she, too, in her heart, felt that real life was better than lessons. She taught me, one of my cousins, and two girls who lived near us, according to a pleasant system (still practised, I believe) by which we never worked for longer than twenty-five minutes at a time on any subject for fear of tiring young intelligences. Lessons often consisted of looking at smudgy reproductions of pictures by Pre-Raphaelites, then describing them. I was good at this and have loved irises and lilies ever since. When part of the syllabus proved dull—'citizenship,' for example, contained in a book with a dreary blue cover and crossheads printed in a clumsy bold type face—Ursula let it fade out and gave us essays on 'My Best Day's Hunting' to write instead. She was ruthless about good sense and good manners, though, and she did us good.

When the bank's lack of sympathy finally drove me to school (can it really have been cheaper than governesses, or had I become so uppish by then that they felt I needed it?), the headmistress told my mother that she had never before encountered a girl so badly grounded. I felt indignant on Ursula's behalf, but it was probably the truth. She enjoyed the things that we enjoyed too much, and skimped the rest. She must have reported me intelligent, because even in her day it was understood that I would be the one to go to Oxford, but what, apart from my lust for reading and my facility for 'essays,' led her to that conclusion, I now find it hard to see. I cannot remember employing my mind, at that time, on any subject other than horses and sex.

4

M Y PARENTS' IDEAS on bringing up children (or rather
my mother's, for my father was not much interested and
left it to her), were slightly more progressive than those of
the rest of the family. Sex was a distasteful subject to all of them, but
I believe my mother would have given us honest answers if we had
asked questions. She would have been embarrassed, though, and
we knew it, so we did not ask. I cannot remember her telling me of
any aspect of it except menstruation, which she did not describe as
connected with the tricky subject of childbirth, but only as a boring
thing which happened to women and, luckily, did not hurt. She
got out of giving us 'little talks' or one of those hygienic handbooks
for the young by letting us run loose with a lot of animals and for-
bidding us no book, however 'grown-up.' With this freedom, she
believed, we would soon know all about it and, knowing all, would
develop a healthy attitude towards it: which, in her terms, would
have meant forgetting it. On the same principle, when I was older,
she imposed no chaperonage on me but allowed me to come and
go with my young men unchecked, hoping that trust would breed

reliability. She was aware of the increasing freedom of the 'twenties, she had come to see her own upbringing as absurdly strait-laced, but she was at that stage of emancipation where it is believed that it can be applied to manners without affecting morals: a touching stage. 'You know that I trust you,' she would sometimes say, nervously. I was always grateful for this attitude, partly for its generosity, partly because its consequences were not what she expected.

Animals unaided did not do the trick. At eight or ten years old you can know all about bitches coming on heat, and how a bull mounts a cow, without connecting it with human beings. It was in a book that the odd, almost inconceivable fact that people do what animals do turned up under my hand, as solid as a stone. I think that my mother, in spite of her policy, had *hoped* that we would not chance on Marie Stopes's *Planned Parenthood*—small and black, it was pushed very far back on one of the lower shelves—but chance on it I did, at the age of eleven. Can I really have pulled it out with a slightly cynical amusement at the idea of our parents reading up on how to rear us methodically, which was what the title suggested to me? That is how I remember it.

The diagrams, and the clear descriptions of sexual intercourse, astonished and thrilled me: I had stumbled on the Answer. At first excitement was mixed with dismay—I had seen those awkward, panting, heaving animals: could human beings be so undignified?— but I got over that in a day or two and was soon borrowing Dr Stopes's reverent tone as I explained to Betty, then my closest friend, that it only seemed ugly to us because we did not have husbands: done with one's love it would be beautiful. Lord, but that was a full week! A summer week in the Hertfordshire house, because I remember hurrying through the fence between our paddock and the park round Betty's house, loaded almost to bursting point with information and impatient even of the moment it took to disengage my cotton frock from the brambles which caught at it. First the immense discovery, the reading and rereading, the digesting of the principle of the thing, and then of the fascinating details (it was a good idea to put a towel under your hips to keep the sheets clean—years later my first lover was much tickled when I got into bed for my deflowering equipped with a towel); then the complicated shift of focus, the act of faith almost, by which I converted what was dismaying into what was desirable.

According to the sort of theory half-held by my mother, that should have settled that: fully informed, Betty and I should have relapsed into thinking only of our animals, our games and our lessons, with sex pigeonholed until the time came for it. Instead, intoxicated by our discovery of what was clearly the most exciting thing in life, we rarely thought or spoke of anything else from the day I first read the book to the time, a couple of years later, when Betty's mother found one of my letters to her daughter and forbade the continuance of the friendship on the grounds that I was a dirty-minded little girl. This was unfair. I had access to more information than Betty had, but her interest in it was no less avid than mine. It was also humiliating, but one of the reasons that I believe my mother was prevented from helping us about sex more by shyness than by a fundamentally prudish attitude towards it is that she comforted me in my shame by taking the incident in a matter-of-fact way: it did not seem to surprise her that we had discussed such things—she did not consider me a monster, as I had half expected her to.

Marie Stopes taught me the facts; anonymous English ballad writers confirmed my belief that they were pleasures. The spring following my initiation we went, as usual, to stay at Beckton. My grandmother never allowed anyone else to spring-clean my grandfather's books: each year, with a scarf tied over her hair, she would spend weeks going through the shelves—clap-clap, a flick with a duster, then a quick polish to already gleaming bindings with some unguent prepared from an antiquary's recipe. She was doing the smoking-room one day, kneeling on the floor among stacks of books while I lolled on the sofa. 'What are those?' I asked idly, reaching for the top volume of a pile of six lovely ivory-coloured books with the one word 'Ballads' gleaming on their spines. I felt smug at asking. Ballads, I knew, were the kind of poem one ought to like best at my age, but I usually found them dull and preferred Elizabethan conceits or eighteenth-century elegancies ('Cupid and my Campaspe played/At cards for kisses' was one of my favourites). 'You wouldn't enjoy those,' said my grandmother too quickly, and added, half to herself, 'Horrible things, I can't think how they got here.' ('Men!' she must have been thinking.)

I was on to it at once, put back the volume I had picked up, and talked of something else. That evening I sneaked down, took one of the books at random, and carried it off to my bedroom.

The first poem I read was a long one, and dull, but it was about the gelding of the devil so it had its anatomical passages. Others were far more exciting. The collection was an orgy of rustic bawdy, full of farting and pissing and sex spelt out, embalmed in an atmosphere of guffawing, leering naughtiness. I went through four of the volumes in a fever, hiding them in my underclothes drawer, for in some ways children are as trusting as adults and it did not occur to me that they would be found there. They were, of course. The strange thing, considering how little we did for ourselves in the way of folding up or putting away, was that it did not happen sooner. No one said anything about it—they felt, I suppose, that the incident should be played down rather than up—but when I went to fetch the fifth volume, the whole set had gone. My sense of deprivation was violent; not far, I am sure, from what an alcoholic would feel if his secret stock of whisky was discovered and removed.

Those poems gave me physical sensations of excitement, which *Planned Parenthood* had not done. Flushed and wriggling, searching greedily back and forth for the sexiest passages, I must have been a displeasing sight as I read them. If, now, I found a little girl reading those books in that way, my impulse would be to stop her doing it. But I do not think it did me any harm. 'Dirty-minded' Betty's mother thought me, and dirty-minded I was, doing furtively what I felt to be wrong, but what is the dirty-mindedness of adolescents? Where does it come from, in families where the parents have made no attempt to force their children to think in such terms?

There are always the nuances of behaviour which betray adults' reactions to things whatever their rational policy may be; nuances picked up by children with infallible accuracy. There is always the sense of taboo which comes from silence. And there are always the effects of experiences connected with excretion—'dirty little girl' over a wetted bed, or merely an adult's expression of distaste over a smelly chamberpot (or one's own distaste over it)—to attach an idea of dirtiness to anything belonging to the private parts of the body. But beyond these things there is something else which no attitude, however 'wholesome,' can be sure of getting round: the fact that sex is an *activity*. To learn about it, then put it in cold storage—it is not so simple as that. Learn about sex, and you want, if it has not been deliberately smeared for you, to *act* it; and while, according to the mores of the society in which you live, you are too young for that, you must inevitably go through a period of tension and frustration. 'Dirty-mindedness' is the way—or one of the ways—in which this tension relieves itself, and what is so dreadful about that? 'Laughter of the wrong sort,' as a woman I knew called the titters released in classrooms by paintings of the nude, is not a charming sound, but it is a harmless substitute for illegitimate babies bred between teenage children. I dislike the picture of myself reading those ballads, but I do not wish that I had never done so.

Perhaps children who act it out by masturbating spend less time thinking about sex than I did. If I had known of the activity I should certainly have indulged in it, but I did not know of it, and not having a strong practical bent, I did not invent it. I doubt whether it would have made much difference. Physically precocious as I happened to be, I was bound to go through an obsessed stage; and having been spared neurotic extremes in my parents' attitude I was not likely to be damaged by it. I believe now that the way a person feels about sex, once he has struggled through adolescence, depends largely on other things than his 'sex education': on, for example, his imagination, his honesty, his capacity for tenderness, and his ability to comprehend the 'reality' of other people. Those are the things to fret about, rather than the little horror's passion for looking up rude words in the dictionary or peeping through keyholes.

Absorbing though my obsession with sex remained throughout my teens, it stayed in a watertight compartment: it did not leak out, or hardly leaked out, into my relationship with boys. From the age of nine to the age of fifteen, right through the hot early stages of the fever, I was protected by being in love with a boy of my own age, for the reason that he was kind, gentle, brave, honest, and reliable: the

most rational love of my life. In my daydreams he and I would rescue each other from appalling perils in order to melt together in an
endless kiss; but in real life I should have been astounded if he had so
much as pecked my cheek—something unthinkable: the nearest he
came to expressing affection was to tell his mother that I was a good
sport. Only once did a glimmer of true sexual feeling occur. At the
end of a violent afternoon spent sliding down a haystack, he came
panting up and flopped beside me. 'How red and sticky he looks,' I
thought, with what I expected to be distate—and suddenly, strongly,
wanted to feel that hot cheek against mine. I recognized what was
happening. 'So *that*,' I thought with surprise, 'is what it is really like!'
and I felt adult for having experienced it—adult and secretive. It was
not among the things on which I reported in my ill-fated correspon-
dence with Betty.

5

'GOOD EVENING. . . . Oh, my god, it's Paul's girl!'

'Maggie, you recognized me!'

'Recognized you? Of course I recognized you.'

Maggie held my arm for a moment after kissing me, looking as though she might cry, while I stood there feeling a curious internal vertigo. It was almost twenty years since I had last gone through the narrow door into the taproom of the Plough at Appleton, a small village about ten miles from Oxford; almost twenty years since Maggie and I had seen each other.

I had returned to it by chance. An Oxford friend not seen for years had come home to England with his family on leave. The village in which he had rented a house happened to be Appleton, and he had asked me to stay for a week-end. He had once known me very well, and remembered that it had been 'my' village although by the time I had met him I had become unwilling to visit it again because it was the place to which I had always gone with Paul. To my dismay, this friend was delighted that now, when everything was safely distant, he could be my escort along two hundred yards of country lane into such a significant patch of my past. It was the sort of thing which he himself enjoyed—he was a great man for pious pilgrimages, for gently melancholy evocations of youthful emotion. I had not thought of Maggie's for a long time and was horrified to feel such a violent revulsion from his sentimental kindness. It seemed to me a shocking intrusion on something which had nothing to do with him, and if a refusal would not have been even more sentimental than the visit, I would have been guilty of that rudeness.

And Maggie looked just the same; or perhaps as though she were having one of her 'bad days' after a thick Guinness evening, only now it was twenty years, not a hangover, that made her look like that. When I saw that she, too, did not know what to say, it was almost intolerable. It had taken a long time, but the whole thing had at last been put away as though behind a glass door—always there to be looked at, it need no longer be felt. But standing there in the taproom, with Maggie's hand on my arm. . . . 'Oh, my god, it's Paul's girl!' Of course I was. And yet finally, conclusively, forever, I was not. So vision skidded and squinted into dizziness.

Paul began long before the days when we went to Maggie's. When I was fifteen my parents decided to employ a tutor during the holidays, to cram my brother for the entrance examination to his public school. They offered the job to the son of a friend of theirs, who was at Oxford, and he, unable to take it, recommended a fellow undergraduate whom he knew to have run out of money and to be looking for a way of earning some. I was beginning to find my pure and unrequited love for the boy who thought me a good sport too quiet for my taste, so I fell in love in advance, first with the friend's son, then, when I heard that Paul was coming instead of him, with Paul. If he had been ugly or shy or snubbing I might have fallen out of love again when he appeared, but he was none of these things, so within two days the lines of my life were laid down.

I wrote to a friend of mine: 'The tutor's come, and he's a perfectly marvellous person. He's got brown eyes and fair hair and I suppose he ought to be taller really but he has got broad shoulders and a good figure, and he's country and London at the same time. He would be at home anywhere. He's very funny and he reads a lot, but he isn't a bit highbrow. We took a boat up the stream yesterday, through all that tangly bit beyond the wood, like going up the Amazon, and he made up a tremendous story about who we were and what we were doing. He knows more about birds than anyone I know, but he dances well too.'

Paul was very much as I described him. Fair-skinned myself, I am rarely attracted by fair people, but he, in spite of hair which in summer would bleach into golden streaks as though he had perox-ided it, had an almost Latin pigmentation: sherry-coloured eyes and a matt skin which went with the compact, smooth cut of his features. He was commonsensical and quick-witted rather than clever, good-humoured and high-spirited rather than witty, but the distinc-tions were not at that time perceptible to me. He was confident, a charmer, and was considered by some of his elders and by more sober young men to be slightly delinquent because he was rarely out of money trouble and would make love to any willing woman, even though she might be the wife or daughter of a friend.

His chief quality—the thing I hit on with 'he would be at home anywhere,' the thing for which I most loved him, the thing which influenced me, I now gratefully believe, more than any other quality in any other person—was that he went like steel to magnet for the essence of any person, place, activity, or situation, working from no preconception or preferred framework. He had his own touchstone for what he called 'genuineness,' his own unformulated laws which determined whether people were 'real' or not. This eager acceptance of diversity of experience was immensely exciting to me, and of great value, coming as it did when I was ready to take any imprint which came my way. I had reached the stage of being vaguely and for the most part privately in opposition to the laws governing my family's outlook, but it was not a strong or reasoned opposition because there was not enough to oppose: I loved my family and my home, and I enjoyed all the things we did. It was Paul, with his simply expressed but passionately felt dicta—'The great thing to remember is to *take people as they come*'; 'I hate people who aren't *natural* in any situation'—who broke down my conditioning and made me anxious to meet people as people, regardless of class or race: a freedom from shackles which did not then chafe me, but which would probably have become locked on me, for which I shall always thank him.

Paul used to boast of his 'sense of situation' and his 'way with people.' It was because he felt his way through life with such whiskers that he became at once a member of the household at the Farm. He enjoyed the place and us as we felt we should be enjoyed; he steered clear of the divergencies that might have alienated my parents; and he plunged happily into the 'situation' of moulding admiring youth as he felt it ought to be moulded. As far as I can remember he managed to hammer a certain amount of information into my brother's then resolutely closed mind, but chiefly he concentrated on opening our eyes to Life.

His family lived in London but spent most of each summer on the coast not far from us, where they had a cottage. His father was a businessman and, without being rich, had more money than mine.

Paul had gone to Eton; my brother was going to Wellington. Paul, if his father had his way, would leave Oxford for a job in some organization like I.C.I. or Unilever; my brother, unless he developed some strong bent in another direction, would probably end up like my father, in the Army. Anyone who lived in London and who made money as Paul's father did (he sometimes lost it, too), by knowing what went on in the Stock Exchange, seemed to us so dashing as to be almost disreputable, while anyone who lived in the country and either just *had* money or, failing that, earned a salary seemed to them so salt-of-the-earth as to be almost dull. In spite of this the two families liked what they knew of each other and no one frowned on the intimacy which soon developed between Paul and me. After that first summer of employment as a tutor, he would come to stay for parties to be my escort, or I would go to stay at the cottage to sail with him and the youngest of his three sisters. She, two years older than he was, became for a time my substitute for Paul, the object on which I focussed my love and admiration, for I had found a letter in his bedroom from a girl with whom he had clearly slept, and this, with the four years between our ages (to fifteen, nineteen is grown-up), had persuaded me that this love, too, must stay unrequited for a time. I was too sensible to hope to compete while still in pig-tails. So deliberately and fairly calmly, hanging about his sister as much as I was able, I settled down to wait.

The best days of that time were spent sailing. There is nothing to beat messing about in boats (well, yes: there is writing and making love and travelling and looking at pictures, but there is nothing *like* it, and it is good). Estuary sailing in a fourteen-foot half-decked cutter of doubtful class but sound performance was what Paul introduced me to, so estuary sailing is the kind I like best. To do more than poke my nose out to sea, while inching along the coast from one river mouth to another, frightens me a little. Sailing on the open sea is surely even better, to those who are accustomed to it, but I remain uneasily aware of how extraordinary it is that so small and frail a man-made contraption as a sailing-boat can survive such gigantic and indifferent opposition. Water I have always loved, but the sea—there is too much of it. Only one thing is more frightening: cloud seen from above, on those hallucinating occasions when it takes the form of landscape. After a flight in such conditions I am haunted by those gullies, those escarpments, those cliff faces and peaks rising out of stretches of eroded desert. I cannot throw off the feeling that I have been watching a *real world*. The common-sense knowledge that if I were to float down on it by parachute I should go through it is bad enough; but worse is the nightmare image of landing on it, finding that it existed, but on unearthly terms—no water, no warmth, no growth—so that I would be the only living thing, with no prospect but to die slowly as I stumbled antlike through a world that was solid but belonged to an eternally foreign order of being. The sea, too, is a world with laws which do not accommodate human life. That human ingenuity has found ways of using it, even of playing with it, is foolhardiness.

But an estuary—from the first shift of shingle under rope soles, the first breath of river-mud smell, I was ready to be at home. The sound made by the planks of a jetty underfoot, the strands of seaweed drying on its piles above water level, unfolding beneath it; the glimpses of water between its planks and the feel of rough iron rings to which dinghies are made fast: I know no purer or simpler pleasure than sitting with legs dangling over the edge of a jetty while someone has gone to fetch the new tiller, or to fill water containers, or (more often) to see the man who is repairing the outboard motor.

The waiting about which attends any sort of boat's motor is the only thing I like about them. In use they are a torment. Chuff chuff chuff—silence. Chuff, a couple of smoke rings, a reek of petrol— silence. 'You'd better go up and take another sounding.' 'There's enough water but we're drifting to port.' 'God damn this bloody bastard.' The absence of a motor can be inconvenient, however, as I learnt when becalmed without one for a whole week on the Clyde, sailing with a man who allowed six inches of weed to flourish on the bottom of his already lumpish boat and who left wet sails huddled in a heap at the end of a day (Paul's ghost asking, 'What on earth are you doing with this frightful chap?').

That boat would hardly come about in anything less than a stiff breeze, and in the few light airs we had each morning it was no more handy than a dead whale. On those light airs, and on tide and current, we meandered slowly about the Clyde, getting stuck at last at an anchorage off a tiny island called the Little Cumbrae, in the middle of an hysterical ternery. The birds felt our presence an outrage the whole day long, their querulous screaming and wheeling turning our idle craft into some ravening sea monster, so that when on the second morning there was a breath of wind it was a relief to put off. A long reach took us to the edge of a sandbank running out from the mainland, and there the wind died. There was a mist. 'I'm going to row to the Great Cumbrae and ask for a tow home,' said the boat's owner—there was a village on the Great Cumbrae. 'You take soundings and anchor when you get between four and three fathoms.' He set off in a vile temper to row for more than a mile, vanishing into the mist after about fifty yards.

It was a thirty-foot boat, everything about it heavy and contrary. After I had got the anchor down I doubted whether it was holding in the sandy bottom, but I could not check whether we were drifting because I could see nothing to check by. Bits of flotsam on the oil-smooth water were certainly moving in relation to the boat, but was it because *they* were being carried on a slow current, or was it because the *boat* was being carried? I could sense the cat-backed sand lying in wait, expected every instant that deceptively gentle stroking sensation which heralds running quietly aground. If we did? I saw myself going overboard into water up to my neck to prop her side against the tide's ebbing with oars and the table-top from the cabin. It would not be the first time I had done it, but I had never done it alone, without help. And supposing a squall struck? Squalls could come up in two minutes out of a dead calm on those mountain-surrounded waters, or so I had repeatedly been told: 'A very tricky estuary, you have to know it well.' I did not know it at all.

I tried to repeat poems to myself, and I tried to summarize the plot of *Emma*—not just what happened, but the exact order in which it happened—but every few minutes I would notice that a particular clot of weed was now floating to the right of the cleat for the jib sheet instead of to its left—that it had crept another six inches towards the stern. After half an hour my hands were sweating, and when something suddenly began to *snort* out of the mist I could feel the blood draining from my face. 'I am going mad!' I thought, until smooth shapes came rolling lazily out of the soft greyness: a couple of porpoises to distract me. They had never come so close before and made me happy for a few moments, but soon they went away again, and then there was nothing but a few invisible birds going over, lamenting like exiled ghosts. When I went below to get a whisky I could hear the rim of the glass clinking against my teeth. A book, I thought, and dug out an Agatha Christie from a mess of rotten cord and baked-bean tins, but could not concentrate. To be so scared is ridiculous, I thought. Even if we *do* run aground. . . . But what if running aground and the squall *happen at the same moment?*

An hour later, back at my flotsam-watching, I heard a new sound: the tap-tap of a rope end against wood. A breeze was coming up. I licked my finger and stuck it in the air: it was coming offshore, off the sandbank. I'll give it five minutes, I thought, but in less than that time it was with me, a decent, steady breeze blowing in a direction which would sail me off that bank without any manœuvring being necessary. I knew that I could do nothing single-handed with that horrible boat but sail her in open water with just the right amount of wind; I had rarely done more than crew for Paul and had always had his vigilant eye on me when I took the tiller, and anyway I was not strong enough to handle this awkward bitch. 'You will probably get in a mess,' I told myself, but I did not care. I would not have sat there another minute for a hundred pounds. I skinned my hands as I hauled the anchor in—her bows swung across the chain—and I fumbled and cursed and even cried as I struggled to get the sails up, but I managed it, felt them fill, heard the popple start under her bows, and off I went.

The breeze remained steady, so I could probably have succeeded in taking her into the harbour of the Great Cumbrae, where, no doubt, I should have fouled several people's moorings and brought shame upon myself, but I had in mind nothing so definite as that intention. Just to be under sail in open water was all I wanted. If I had not met the returning dinghy by pure chance, I might be sailing still. I brought the boat about and picked up her owner very neatly, but he, who had found no tow available, whose hands were raw and whose every muscle was aching, was in no state to appreciate it. It was not, in any way, a successful week, since even before that contretemps we had discovered that we had nothing to say to each other, but it was a week which proved the magic of boats. Displeasing though that one was, frustrating though the weather had been, and uncongenial as the boat's owner and I had found each other, what still lives in my memory (besides the sights and sounds, always a delight) is the sharpening tremor of fear in my nerves and the triumphant discovery that it blew away as soon as I was under sail.

The first time I had stayed with Paul's family in their seaside cottage I ate almost nothing for three days, chewing and chewing on mouthfuls which, I feared, would make me vomit if I swallowed them. Nor could I sleep—or not for one night, anyway. I lay listening to the sea on the shingle while feverish tiredness made the bed rock, and whatever I did to my hands—clenched them, shook them, rubbed them, relaxed them—I could not rid them of a dull ache in the palms. This sensation is one that I have not experienced, now, for many years and will almost certainly never experience again, for what could be exciting enough to send my nerves into such a state? I must have spoken, I suppose, since everyone welcomed me kindly and they always seemed pleased to see me again, but I cannot remember doing anything but listen and watch. Paul at the Farm was familiar and unalarming—I even lectured him, sometimes, with fifteen-year-old solemnity—but Paul with a boat, Paul with his gay, wild, funny, grown-up sister: there was something piratical about them together, they had a careless way of flouting the law under which I still was, they were so sure that their own touchstones made nonsense of the conventions. My complete acceptance of everything they said, my rapt attentiveness to every nuance of their behaviour, flattered them both into adopting me. There was never a cabin boy more eager to stow away on a gallant pirate ship than I was to join those two in whatever they did.

Part of my tension came, of course, from love, but much of it was due to my ignorance of their chief occupation: sailing. Horses were my thing—and horses had taught me all the pitfalls of a sport. I knew well how *damned* was the rider who came to a meet in the wrong clothes, or worse, in clothes too right if his mount or riding was wrong; one shrewed glance at a newcomer and I could size him up, *in* or *out*. The man whose bridle had a coloured browband or who had shaped his horse's tail by clipping instead of pulling; the girl who showed curls on her forehead under her bowler, or who had plaited her horse's mane into more than seven plaits—they got short shrift from me. So thoroughly was I conditioned that I could no more have failed to react to such things than a dog could keep its hackles smooth if a strange dog came in at its front door.

So sailing, I knew, would also have its language, its ritual, its taboos. Like anyone of that age, I greatly minded making a fool of myself, and to do it on Paul's ground, under his eyes, would have been intolerable. I had to lie low, lurk in the undergrowth, all eyes and twitching whiskers, picking up clues. I had enough flair to avoid obvious mistakes. I knew, for instance, that I could not go far wrong in my clothes if I kept them warm, practical, and not showy. But all the rest I had to learn.

I never did learn enough to sail well myself. I was not there often enough, and when I was, my anxiety not to make mistakes kept me too docile so that I concentrated on doing what I was told rather than on working things out for myself. But I learnt that when a flight of dunlin zigzags against a thundery sky it is almost invisible until the birds turn so that for a moment all their bellies are exposed; then it is as though a faint streak of white lightning ran across the clouds. I learnt the gait of oyster catchers, the arrowy flight of terns, the ways in which water ruffles, goes sullen, or flashes with what were called locally 'tinkling cymbals'—those neat points of light reflected from every ripple. I learnt that when you wake up at night on a boat anchored far out from the shore, you sometimes hear people *walking* round it, and that when you tip a bucket of water overboard in the darkness, with luck a plunge of white flame will go showering into the depths. I learnt the creakings and patterings, the strainings and shudderings of boats, the gentle winging of sailing before the wind, the clatter of going about, the hissing and ripping of tacking. And I learnt the comfortable silences of two people sailing together, out of which, in the relaxed moments, you say whatever comes into your head. It was an intermittent apprenticeship in sharing profound pleasure.

Ashore, when I was a little older, we would drink beer and eat oysters or bread and cheese with pickled onions in small, dark pubs. I found that I could play darts fairly well—an agreeable surprise for someone with as little co-ordination between hand and eye as I have, to whom games were a mortification. There was a technique in getting in on a game of darts, or in getting accepted at all, for that matter. 'Foreigners,' meaning people who have not been established locally for several years, are distrusted in East Anglia, and the comfortable gossip of watermen and farm labourers over their pints would stop when we came in. Usually when they saw that it was 'old Paul' (everyone there is old, even a 'little old baby'), they would greet us with pleasure, for he had been about those parts for some years and was known to be 'all right,' but even so it would have been a mistake to push in too eagerly, especially for a girl. Pub manners, on which Paul was an expert, demanded quietness, deference to whatever elder, male or female, was installed in 'his' or 'her' corner, familiarity (but not a *display* of familiarity) with water and country, and an appearance of being at ease without an impertinent assumption of being at home. After a while the presence of the well-behaved 'foreigner' would be forgotten by the people who were always there, then remembered again, but in a different way: 'Anyone want a game of darts—what about the young lady?'—and we were off. If I were playing well—if, as on one triumphant occasion, I opened the game with plunk plunk, a double twenty—then we were off into celebration and festivity as well as acceptance. And nothing gave these times more flavour than the knowledge that I would have them to remember when I got back to school.

6

FOR I DID have to go to school soon after we had 'lost our money' and retreated to the Farm. I had been there a term or two by the time Paul came to us. I had not wanted to go, but I had been too ignorant of school life to dread it as I ought. As most adults accept a disagreeable climate, or a dull job, or illness, so children accept the conditions of life wished on them by adults: not willingly, but with fatalism.

As schools go, it was a good school, and I knew as much even at the time. I was also prepared to believe that it would do me good, for at home I had begun to earn accusations of 'uppishness,' 'sulks,' and 'superiority' which I had not enjoyed. I had only been unable to see what I should do to stop earning them. If school would 'rub the corners off' me, as people said it would, if it would 'teach me to get on with other girls,' then good luck to it. But I was not able, and did not see why I should be expected, to go beyond resigned endurance, and enjoy it.

It was a small school looking out over the North Sea. There

must, somewhere, have been some kind of land mass between its playing fields and the North Pole, but it did not feel as though there was: in winter the sweat falling from your brow as you ran after a lacrosse ball (you never caught that ball if you were me) all but turned to icicles before it reached the ground. Irritatingly, the rigorous climate and our constant exposure to it, both outdoors and in, really were very healthy, so that no one there ever had an infectious disease and only twice was I able to escape into the civilized privacy of the sickroom.

I was fourteen when I first set foot on the loose gravel made from small beach pebbles and went through the elaborate porch of white woodwork into that smell of polish, ink, and gym shoes; fourteen when I arrived, and almost eighteen when I left. A lifetime, it seemed. Good God, think only of one summer term! No stretch of time has ever looked so endless as those *thirteen weeks* before I had been able to black out one single day on my calendar. Three or four years ago I was walking down Oxford Street when I saw a shop-window display of school uniforms, trunks, and tuck boxes backed by a huge mockery of a school-child's calendar, the days blacked out up to the current date, crowned by the monstrous legend 'Only Five More Days to the *Beginning* of Term.' . . . I stared at it in incredulous horror. Whoever designed that display can only have heard of boarding schools, never have been at one, for how could anyone who had experienced it forget the despair under the stolid endurance with which one crept forward, square by tiny square, towards that red-embellished date which meant freedom regained?

Apart from games, the things I had to do at school were not

objectionable. Lessons I saw as necessary, often interesting, and sometimes enjoyable; I made friends whose companionship I appreciated. It was the *absence* of things which had to be endured: the absence of freedom, the absence of home, the absence of privacy, the absence of pleasures. When I understood that not for one minute of the day could I be alone, except in the lavatory, and that every minute had its ordained employment, my spirit shrivelled.

During my first term, when it was all strange as well as barbarous, I used to employ talismans. There was a thrush which sang outside my dormitory in the mornings, whose fountain of song, a voice from the outside world, I listened to so avidly that I learnt to recognize the bird's recurrent phrases. One of them, in particular, seemed like a promise, and I could get up more easily once I had heard it. Our cubicles in the dormitories were surrounded by white curtains hung on rails. At least, I thought, I can keep them pulled round my bed and *imagine* that I am alone. But on the first evening the monitor explained kindly that once we were undressed we must pull the curtains back. I did so, got into bed, and lay staring through tears at the band which held the curtains to a hook in the wall. One of the brass rings on the end of the band was squashed into an oval shape. I invested that ring with friendly powers, gave it a name—Theodore—and would touch it before going to sleep. Nobody else could know about it, nobody could guess at something so absurd, so the ring at least was something privately mine and could transmit little messages of reassurance. All through my schooldays, even when I was established and secure and had won an unusual number of freedoms by a mixture of luck, determination, and suppleness in accepting the role of 'a character,' I maintained a private stable of symbols to keep me in touch with outside. Chrysanthemums were one. They smelt of the dance my grandmother gave for us every Christmas, always called 'Diana's dance' because my birthday fell at that time. There was a blue bowl in my headmistress's sitting room the beauty of which I chose to think was noticed by no one else; there were the frogs making slow and shameless love in the lily pond; there was Rufty, the matron's fat, cross smooth-haired fox terrier. These things would catch my eye as I went from class to class, or came in from the playing fields, and would say, 'Patience, outside hasn't stopped existing.' But no talisman was more comforting than the knowledge that I, anonymous as I might seem in my blue serge gym tunic and my black shoes with straps over the instep, was the girl who had played darts with Paul, Hooky Jimson, and old Gooseberry King in the back bar of the Swan. And after Paul had kissed me for the first time. . . . 'I am ashamed of you,' said my headmistress. 'You are an intelligent girl, you can work when you want to. These marks are the result of feckless idleness.' I looked back at her serene and unmoved. Arrows of shame were in the air, all right, but all I had to do was to say to myself, 'Last holidays Paul kissed me,' and they melted away.

It was at school that my secret sin was first brought into the open: laziness. I was considered a clever girl, but lazy. It has been with me ever since, and the guilt I feel about it assures me that it is a sin, not an inability. It takes the form of an immense weight of inertia at the prospect of any activity that does not positively attract me: a weight that can literally paralyse my moral sense. That something *must* be done I know; that I *can* do it I know; but the force which prevents my doing it when it comes to the point, or makes me postpone it and postpone it until almost too late, is not a conscious defiance of the 'must' nor a deliberate denial of the 'can.' It is an atrophy of the part of my mind which can perceive the 'must' and 'can.' I slide off sideways, almost unconsciously, into doing something else, which I like doing. At school, with my algebra to prepare and a half-hour of good resolutions behind me, I would write a poem or would reach furtively behind me for a novel out of the communal study's bookshelf, by which they were foolish enough to give me a desk. It was a year before they understood that no amount of scolding or appealing to reason would cure me of this habit, and moved me to a desk from which I could not reach the shelf unobserved. I do the same sort of thing today, at the age of forty-two. I may have advertising copy to prepare. The copy date comes nearer—it is on me—it is *past* . . . and I find myself dictating a letter to an author telling him how much I enjoyed his newly submitted book. So often have I proved that this form of self-indulgence ends by making my life less agreeable rather than more so that my inability to control it almost frightens me; but that I should ever get the better of it now seems, alas, most unlikely.

Once my headmistress had sized me up, she used to deal with it by savaging me once a term, at a well-judged moment about two weeks before the end-of-term examinations. 'Diana—she wants you in her study.' With my heart in my boots and my record only too clear in my head I would trail along the dark corridor and tap at her door. She would be standing in front of her fireplace, wearing one of her brown or bottle-green knitted suits, hitching the skirt up a little, perhaps, to warm the backs of her legs. 'Miss Beggs tells me . . . Miss Huissendahl tells me . . . ' and the shameful evidence would be put before me in a voice of such disgust, with such ponderous sarcasm, that I could have hit her. Almost in tears with resentment and humiliation, I would go back to the study and defiantly read a novel or write letters all through the next preparation period—but mysteriously, when the examinations came, my marks would be adequate. After a couple of years of this ritual I should have been dismayed if she had skipped it, for I liked to do well. I remember feeling indignant one term, when she left it until too late so that the only subject in which I came top was English. That I came top in anyway, because I liked it.

Even my headmistress, however, could not inject adequacy in mathematics. At the sight of figures I became, and still become, imbecile; and this is a block so immovable that I do not feel guilt at it—there is nothing I can do about it. What set it up I do not know. My first lessons in arithmetic, given by a beloved aunt, I remember with pleasure. We played with matchsticks and it made sense. But once I had mastered adding, subtracting, and dividing I reached a point beyond which nothing could make me go. So profound is my aversion to the symbols of number that I cannot even trust myself to number the pages of a typescript with any reliability: I will find on looking back over it that I have written '82, 83, 84, 76, 77.' Recognizing a hopeless case when they saw one, my teachers recommended that I should drop mathematics and take one of the permitted substitute subjects for the obligatory School Certificate examination of my day—botany, it was. I enjoyed dissecting black-berries and the heads of poppies and then making drawings of them, and was so thankful to be relieved of those nightmare numbers that I did quite well in it.

I do not regret knowing nothing about mathematics, but I am sorry that I had another, slightly less serious block about Latin, and I believe that it could have been undermined. If, after the barest minimum of grammar had been taught me, I had been let loose with a dictionary and, say, Ovid's *Ars Amatoria*. . . . But oh, how badly Latin used to be taught! Those nameless girls, constantly making presents of goats to that boring queen! I used to hang on to the goats for all I was worth—I liked goats, goats interested me immensely—but they were never allowed to do anything in the least goatlike, so it was no good. I tried hard with Latin. If there was a choice of verbs to learn I would pick the ones which meant something to me, such as 'to dance,' 'to ride,' 'to drink'—and, of course, 'to love'—and I found that the future tense, which could be used as an incantation, stayed with me fairly well. 'I will dance, you will dance, he will dance'—pause to dream about 'he'—'we will dance—I shall be wearing a dress with a huge skirt of shell-pink tulle—no, heavy gold lamé, perhaps—and he will. . . . ' Even more memorable was the form 'Let him love.' 'Let him love!'—my hair, for that scene, would have had to go raven black. . . . I struggled through the school examinations; with stubborn holiday coaching from an elderly clergyman I survived the entrance examination for Oxford, and once there, with more extra coaching, I got through the first-year examination known as Pass Mods. And then, having spent all those years on it, having learnt what must have amounted to quite a *lot* of it, with one great 'Huff!' of relief I blew the whole language out of my mind. The only words of Latin I know today are a few future tenses and *veni, vidi, vici.*

In the Hall of my school, used as a chapel and for all communal occasions, there was, and I suppose still is, a board carrying the names of all the head girls. Mine (and this still seems to me very odd) is on it, which only goes to show how closely biographers should examine evidence. I had been there a long time by then, and had made myself comfortable. By having my appendix removed I had been excused games for all of one term, and the headmistress was tactful enough never to withdraw this blissful dispensation (perhaps the games mistress implored her not to) so that while others were thumping about after balls, I could go for walks. Once in the sixth form, I was free to sit in the little library instead of in the communal study, and attempts to stop me going to bed at eight-thirty, with the little ones, had long been abandoned. The point of that was that the little ones were too much in awe of me to bang on the bathroom door. I could lie alone in hot water for as much as ten minutes at a time (and Blanche Dubois was no more addicted to hot baths than I was while suffering school), and once in bed I might have, if I was lucky, a precious half-hour in an empty room. To begin with, a few girls had been mildly unkind to me for being bad at games and reading so much, but the two things had now become part of my public persona, funny and rather engaging. I was good-tempered and obliging, and had an easily won reputation as a wit: I could feel that people liked me. I expected my last year at school to be almost pleasant, particularly as School Certificate was behind me and I was specializing in English, my best subject, in preparation for Oxford.

It had not occurred to me that *everyone else had left*. Like flotsam stranded by a receding tide, there remained of the senior girls only myself and a large, kind, dull girl called Jennifer. The departing sixth form had to go through an almost parliamentary procedure for electing the new head girl, and after their session an anxious delegation came to me as I peacefully read *Sparkenbrooke* in the library, and said, 'We are awfully sorry, we know that you will hate it—but Jennifer *can't* be head girl—you can see that, can't you? So we *had* to elect you.'

'Nonsense,' I said. 'I won't do it. You can't make me if I don't want to.' They pleaded for a little while, then went away to ask the headmistress what they should do. While I waited, I examined my feelings. Horror had been my first reaction, but after that, had I been putting it on a little, was I not faintly pleased, underneath, at the prospect of such eminence? With immense smugness I decided that I was amused, yes, but *not* pleased: I really was a girl who so despised everything to do with school that nothing would persuade her to accept.

Then the old woman stumped in and said, 'Come into the garden.' She put her arm through mine and walked me briskly up and down among the roses, chuckling and saying flattering things like 'Look, you've got enough sense to see that all this is quite unimportant, but it would make life easier for me if you accepted.' I was fond of her by then. She had once nearly expelled me and had shouted, 'Have you no moral sense at all?' to which I had shouted back 'None, if that's what you call moral sense,' so we had battle scars to share. Soon I was arguing to myself 'Ah, why make so much fuss, it's not worth it,' but a secret feeling of importance was swelling in me. I made my own terms. I would have nothing to do, I said, with the head girl's traditional responsibility towards games (making up teams and so on); Jennifer must do that. All right, she said, and I accepted. And I did not feel ashamed. I still felt amused, and I did not feel *very* pleased, but I did, alas, feel a *little* pleased. I had shown that I did not want it, and now I had got it; I had made my little omelette, and it was not ungratifying to find the eggs still there.

I can truthfully say, however, that by the end of that short spell as queen of a tiny castle I came back to my first frame of mind. The very fact that I could from time to time feel myself becoming slightly corrupted by an apparent eminence—feeling self-satisfied, when no one knew better than I did how little reason there was for self-satisfaction—ended by confirming me in a native indifference to matters of status. It was all a lot of nonsense, I concluded, and whenever since then I have been in situations where official status was held to be important, I have continued to find that true.

On my last day of school, Packing Day, the day of joy, the day when we stayed up late after fruit salad for supper and sang, heaven knows why, the Eton Boating Song and Harrow's 'Forty-Years On,' I looked down from my heights at the cheerfully bellowing crowd of girls and thought, 'Now perhaps—yes, surely—you will feel a moment of regret that it is ending?' But I did not. I knew that I had learnt a lot there, had made some good friends and had some amusing times. I remembered lying flat on my back on the big table in the middle of the study, so overcome by laughter that I thought they would have to carry me up to bed. I remembered drawing lessons in the summer garden, and playing the part of Mr Badger in *Toad of Toad Hall*. I remembered standing for Labour in the mock election we had run at the time of a real one (my grandmother sent my opponent a bundle of Conservative literature as ammunition). I had not, after my first two terms, been unhappy except when in trouble through my own fault—I had even enjoyed a lot of it. But never, for, a single day, had I been doing anything but wait for it to end and now it had ended. Thank God.

7

THAT I STOOD as Labour candidate in the school's mock election when all my family were unquestioning Conservatives was partly the result of Paul's influence, partly of my headmistress's. Paul was more or less apolitical, but he had jolted me out of conformity with my family's mores. He was anti-Them. Particularly he was, as an undergraduate, disgusted by standards of material success which threatened to involve him in the kind of career he would detest. His father hoped that he would settle down as a Man in a Grey Flannel Suit, and of that, by temperament, he was the antithesis. He talked of most conservative conventions as tedious or funny and of some of them as immoral, and since, at that stage, whatever he said was Revealed Truth to me, rebellion rather than conformity inevitably became my line. It went with the modern poetry to which he had introduced me. His first present to me, some time in my fifteenth year, had been the complete works of Oscar Wilde and T. S. Eliot's collected poems, and while the Wilde had been just my cup of tea, the Eliot had been champagne. It was a brilliant present, coming from someone not himself a great reader of poetry ('I don't understand much of this,' he wrote in it, 'but I expect you will. Love, Paul'), but he had a flair for present-giving. Nonchalantly but neatly he pushed me into a kind of reading of which I knew nothing but for which I was ripe.

Whether my headmistress voted Liberal or Labour I do not know, but she and her sisters, one felt, had spent their distant youth in earnest concern for women's rights or the reform of education and the prison system: she came of a family with a good old-fashioned radical tradition, she was a pacifist, and she saw to it that the school library was salted with pacifist and Left Wing reading. She made no overt attempts to influence her pupils politically, seeing her task as that of teaching us to think for ourselves (not to mention that of retaining the confidence of our parents), but one of the reasons why she liked me in spite of my shortcomings was that in so far as I thought at all, my thinking went in what seemed to her the right direction. The national newspapers and the weeklies were always spread on a long table in the school's entrance hall; we were not forced to read them, but we were encouraged to. In the 'thirties anyone who had had her shell cracked for her and was not a moron could hardly read the papers without veering to the left. By the time I finished school I was an imperfectly informed but convinced socialist, pacifist, and agnostic.

My agnosticism did not have my headmistress's blessing, though, true to her principles of non-intervention in matters of conscience, she took no action when I stopped taking Communion. I had been brought up as a member of the Church of England, liking God. He knew everything about me but he was Love and he was Understanding, so it would be hard to do anything for which he would not forgive me. In the book of Bible stories from which my grandmother read to us on Sundays, he was a figure of benevolence manifesting himself in a landscape remarkable for its beautiful sunsets, and later, in the Bible itself and in Beckton Church (as familiar and beloved as the morning-room), he was a less material, more complex development of the same spirit. I have friends who turned their backs on the churches in which they were brought up because of the churches' irrational rigours; I was able to drift out of mine so easily because of its mildness.

The early vision of meaningless chaos beyond the rim of human experience with which I had confronted my dismayed grandmother had come to me, as far as I can recall, unprompted. It is echoed in the sensations given me by cloud landscapes, and was crystallized in an experience I had when going under an old-fashioned anaesthetic at the age of sixteen, when I had my appendix out. As a small child I had known the usual terror, no worse than anyone else's, of *things* under my bed. I had readily accepted that these monsters were imaginary and was not troubled by them for long, but while I was going under the anaesthetic, one of them came out and killed me. I had lost consciousness, then regained it, perhaps because the anaesthetist had reduced the flow too soon. Opening my eyes in a strange white room, I had not the least idea where I was, why I was there—the strong white light seemed to be that of terror at my helpless ignorance of my situation. Then something came down over my face and I knew in a flare of horror that it was a claw—the claw of the monster who *had* been under the bed all the time, in spite of what they had said. Now it had come out and got me, and in a moment I would be dead. I pitched over the edge of a cliff and began to roll down into blackness, gasping to myself, 'They were lying, they were lying!' I got a fingerhold on the cliff and clung to it frantically, knowing that once I could hold on no longer I would be gone—gone into what I expected to be nothingness. But as I peered into the blackness I saw that it was worse than that, it was not nothingness. In cold, absolute horror I saw that the endless night was full of moving shapes, galaxies of dim light circling and interweaving *according to laws of their own* which I, *by my very nature,* could never understand. I thought that I was screaming aloud 'At least let me change!' but I could feel conclusively that I was not going to change. I would have to let go of that cliff and plunge into this new order of being, equipped with nothing but my usual, totally inadequate self. It occurred to me that I might start believing in God, and that if I did it might work—it might give me whatever faculties were needed—but at the same moment I felt it so shameful to clutch at belief simply because I was *in extremis* that I could not bring myself to do it. So in desolation and despair I let go, and down I went.

I did not draw any conclusions from these experiences, nor did I consciously relate them to my religious belief, or lack of it, but I suppose they were symptoms of an innate sense that God was not so simple as man invented him; that if there was a God, he did not necessarily exist to answer man's questions and smooth his way, as did the kindly God of whom I had been taught. The older I grew and the more I read of what was happening in the world, the less likely that seemed, but when I started to attend confirmation classes I was still assuming that in this matter 'they' were more likely to be right than I was, still expecting that with further instruction my doubts would vanish.

The clergyman who came to the school twice a week to prepare us was a gentle, ascetic-looking man of obvious goodness and subtle intelligence. He was better at talking to us about Plato than about Christ, which made me admire him, but at the same time his burnt-out face was that of a man moved more by the spirit than by intelligence: he clearly felt the real object of his classes to be more important than the interesting ideas with which he adorned them. I liked him and admired him, and was impressed by the picture he gave of the Protestant Christian faith. It was beautiful, I could see. It was something to which, if you believed in it, you would have to dedicate your whole life as this man had done—indeed, to believe in it and *not* to dedicate your whole life, *not* to give all you had to the poor, *not* to go out among the unenlightened as a guide, would surely be to make a nonsense of it. I was confirmed, and took Communion for the first time. 'You will find it such a *great* help and comfort in times of trouble,' wrote my godmother, but I was ready for more than that. It would not have surprised me if this mystery had tipped the balance of my doubt for good. It would not have surprised me, but it would most definitely have dismayed me: for if I did turn out to believe with all my heart, if as a logical consequence of belief I did have to give all I had to the poor and so on—just think what I would be giving up!

So how can I be sure what was the real cause of the complete lack of meaning which the sacrament had for me? I only know that I took it reverently, thought with concentration of Christ's crucifixion, and came out feeling just the same as I had felt when I went in. I was well enough instructed to know that to expect 'a sign' was absurd, but still I felt let down. Having gone through this I *ought* not, any longer, to be saying to myself things like 'But if it is not really the body and blood of Christ that I have tasted, why all this fuss about it? It is not—of that I am sure. It is a piece of symbolism to remind us, and how can a piece of symbolism be so *holy* as they make this out to be?' It looked as though God had not made up my mind for me, so I would have to make it up for myself.

Time telescopes, so whether it was for weeks or for months that I considered the matter I do not know. I came to the topsy-turvy conclusion that whether I believed or not depended on what I was prepared to do about it. The Ten Commandments, for example, of which confirmation classes had refreshed my memory: would I be prepared—would I be *able*—to keep them? I was having one of my happy interludes in the sickroom while I pondered them, lying there in comfortable solitude with a mild attack of tonsilitis and nothing to distract me. Most of them were easy, but when it came to 'Thou shalt not commit adultery'—I did not need to examine my heart, it was self-evident: the fact must be faced that I was absolutely sure to commit adultery just as soon as I got the chance. So, I thought, slightly awe-struck but also relieved, I do not believe in God.

'Adultery' and 'God' were both, of course, shorthand terms. I knew the technical meaning of adultery, but I meant something different by it: I meant making love, whether married or not—but marriage would not come for years and love I was going to make *soon*. The obsession with sex in the abstract had faded out and been superseded by a wholehearted concentration on love, usually directed upon one man, but if Paul failed me it would be someone else, and too bad for Paul. We never discussed such things at my school, where the standard of purity was so high that we did not even understand the purpose of the rules which maintained it—the curtains drawn back at night, the ban on less than three girls being alone together. I felt that I knew more about sex and men than most of my companions, and thought about them more, but I would have felt it irresponsible and lacking in taste to spread my knowledge. On one thundery afternoon, during dancing class when we were practising stage falls, I lay sprawled on the parquet in my sage-green art-silk tunic and bloomers and my salmon-pink lisle stockings, thinking, 'If a stevedore'—why a stevedore? I am sure I had never met one—'if a stevedore would come and rape me at this minute, I would let him.' It was an incongruous idea to have in that setting and I enjoyed it as such, feeling sorry for my companions, whom I supposed to be innocent of such emotions. As for me, I knew that I was made for love, and love meant love-making, and I was going to bring this two-things-in-one to a blazing consummation (no, not with a stevedore, that was a joke) as soon as possible. God forbade me to do so and I did not—I could not—feel that he was right.

For just as 'adultery' was shorthand, so was 'God.' I meant by the word that God I had been brought up on, the God of the Church of England as revealed to me by my family and teachers. It was his laws that I was going to break, and because of his convenient, English mildness, I was not afraid of breaking them. And because I was not afraid of breaking them, they were not laws. Anything which could be dismissed with such surprising easiness could not be the whole answer.

I have thought of more logical arguments for non-belief since then, and I have still felt no need to replace that God by another one, but I am not so sure that I ever really stopped 'believing.' I suppose I shall have to come back to this later, if I am to understand why I did not shiver after my dying grandmother asked me why she had lived.

8

RENCH TAFFETA, THIN but crisp, striped with a pencil-point black line on the pure evening-sky blue which Mrs Siddons wore when Gainsborough painted her; grey silk velvet, dove-coloured in shadow, silver in light; another grey, corded silk veiled with chiffon, sashed with lemon yellow; more chiffon, pink over pink pearl embroidery on the breasts; more pearls, a trellis of them as a belt: dresses for dancing in! How many hours—weeks, months, years—did I spend thinking about clothes between the ages of fifteen and twenty? Day clothes too, of course, but evening-dresses were the ones which worked a change, making me feel like a mermaid, a swan, a willow tree, making me move differently, making me ready for love. Usually my mother made them for me; a shop dress was at the same time a luxury and (too often) a disappointment. My mother was clever and romantic about them, raiding shops and fashion magazines for ideas, spending far too much on materials, stitching into them, I see now, the gaiety she was not herself enjoying. She was only in her thirties. For what seemed like hours she would keep me standing in the middle of her drawing-room while she fitted me, both of us growing irritable and I never thinking that she might have been making dresses like that for herself. It was by her choice that we were living at the Farm, away from my father except at weekends, and her temperament was such that given her family, her garden, and her animals she could occupy, or appear to occupy, all of herself with energy and conviction. But there was another side to the coin. Not long ago she flipped it over for me, startling me by saying, 'Sometimes I used to wonder if I could bear it another day. No man, no fun, no travel—it was a dreary time.'

The gayest time of my life was a dreary time? I looked back and saw the frightening abyss between parents and their children: that young woman making the best of the situation into which she had stumbled, 'difficult' and contrary, leading her husband a dance but feeling ashamed of it so that she endured her wilful choice of an un-manned country life as a 'punishment,' while I never questioned the front she put up: that was how she *was*. I accepted her thought and work for me, the generosity with which she turned me loose, as though it were her pleasure and my due. And when she lay awake fretting because I was being driven back from a dance by a young man, I held it against her: why, as I crept upstairs, must she always call apologetically, 'Darling, are you back? Was it a good party?' And when she betrayed anxiety as to how I was using my freedom— an anxiety usually suppressed and often justified from her point of view—anger flared in me.

Paul came and went and came again. Sometimes I would not see or hear from him for weeks, then there would be a long letter or a telephone call, he would rattle up the lane on a motor bicycle or in a secondhand car, and we would be off to a party together, or over to the coast for sailing.

He excelled as someone to do things with. When I remember him it is less for what we said to each other (although we always had plenty to say) than for what we did together. If Paul were playing with a dog, his pleasure in its silky ears, its movements and its expression would make the dog more real; if he were driving one of his old cars, his handling of it made the mere act of driving more interesting. Any place that he loved—the place he called Little Japan, for instance, where the flat land on either side of our sailing estuary curved up and fell again to the marshes in a sandy cliff on which grew a few wind-tortured Scotch firs—sprang its nature at me because of his relish. When he went with me to pick primroses one Easter—an annual ritual for the decoration of Beckton Church—he was astonished at my matter-of-fact attitude to the thick cushions of flowers in a certain part of the wood. I took it for granted that primroses grew thickly there—they always did. He, who lived either in London or on the coast, where they did not flourish, *saw* them. He squatted to bury his face in a clump, then laughed and said, 'My God, but they're marvellous. You're like that chap in the poem—a primrose by the river's brim a yellow primrose was to him!' At once the frail, reddish, slightly hairy stalks of the primroses, their delicate petals, the neat funnels of their centres, the young leaves, folded and lettuce-green among the darker, broader old ones, the grouping of each constellation of flowers, their delicious, rain-fresh scent—everything about them became alive.

He was a good illustration of that thing so difficult to explain to anyone who does not know it from experience: the point of participating in such sports as shooting. A good shot, he liked to exercise the skill, but to accompany Paul as he walked a rough shoot was to see that there was more in it than that. Any kind of hunting, whether with a gun or with hounds, brings the hunter into a close intimacy with the country over which he does it. He learns what kind of cover a partridge, for instance, will favour—learns it so intimately that he can almost feel himself crouching under the broad, wet leaves of a field of sugar beet. He knows what weather does to 'his' land, and to its animal inhabitants; he knows smells and textures, the sounds different sorts of fallen leaves make when he walks through them, the feel under his palm of the moss on the damp side of a tree trunk. Because of his pursuit his senses have to be more alert than those of even the most enthusiastic walker, so he takes more in. He has to contend with nature, not merely look at it, wading through heavy land, clambering through thorny hedges, allowing for wind, observing the light—and discovering, of course, as much as possible about the habits of the creatures he is after. People who have always been, as a matter of course, against blood sports often gibe at the sportsman's professed affection for animals, but paradoxical though it may be, it is perfectly true that there is no surer way to identify with an animal than to hunt it. The man who shoots for pleasure only is doing, I myself now believe, something wantonly destructive—but I have no doubt that it is he who knows best *what it is like to be* a hare, a partridge, a pheasant, a pigeon. . . . Paul knew this very well. He got from shooting the same kind of satisfaction that he got from sailing: that of playing with *real* things—water, wind, living creatures. Sailing was the better of the two, because there the game was more even: water and wind can kill *you* if you are not cleverer than they are. But shooting (and hunting, as I could have taught him) has the same power of engaging you more closely than anything but work with nature, with the elements.

His enjoyment and acceptance were as infectious at a theatre or an exhibition of pictures, dancing in a London night club (he took me to my first, finding the last remaining hansom cab in which to see me home) or gossiping in a village pub. I do not think that it was only because I loved him that I found it so, because I often saw other people responding to this quality in him, but no doubt the fact that I had fallen in love with him even before meeting him had made me specially ready to embrace it; and that, in its turn, had made him accept me as an ally from the beginning.

Our relationship developed slowly but steadily. Even after I had left school I would still react to any opinion of Paul's by going through the motions of accepting a Revealed Truth, but I began to find that afterwards I would sometimes blink and have second thoughts. I began to see that being five years older than I was did not prevent him from being young. He had a pontificating vein when he generalized and it was not *lèse-majesté* on my part if it sometimes struck me as funny, or even absurd. If Paul said 'It is *far* safer to drive fast than to drive slowly' I would not go so far as to say at once 'Don't be silly'; I would suppose that it must, in some mysterious way, be true, but later I would come back to the idea and think about it, and reach my own conclusions. Was he, for example, right when he expounded a theory of which he was fond for about a year: that all sexual relationships were basically the pursuit of an essential thrill which, in its purest essence, could only be found in rape? This, he warned me gravely, was why I should find making love with a man who loved me, and therefore could not rape me, a little disappointing. It seemed to me an impressive idea at first, but later I began to wonder if, possibly. . . . I began to tease Paul more often, as well as to argue with him, and his elder-brotherly affection for me was a little modified each time we met.

There were plenty of other young men about—our county was well-endowed in that respect—and I never thought of holding them off for Paul's sake: the gaining of experience was too valuable and exciting in itself to be rejected. He was the man I loved, he was the man I was waiting for, but meanwhile if anyone else wanted to fall in love with me, or to kiss me, or to tell me I was attractive, I would welcome it greedily. It was pure chance that it was, in fact, Paul who kissed me first. By then I had been waiting for him for two years, which anyone over twenty-five should read as five, or eight, or ten, for it seemed an eternity. The vigil, I felt, had earned me recompenses which I was ready to grasp. But it so happened that going to a dance with my cousins, at just seventeen the youngest of the party and ready for anything, I met Paul unexpectedly after one of our gaps and he saw more sharply than he had seen before that I was growing up. He noticed it half-way through the evening, left his own party, and swooped me away from mine.

He took me out to sit in a parked car, put his arm round me and told me a fairy story—he liked to make up stories. I dared not move for fear that he would think I was uncomfortable, which I was, and take his arm away. When we were dancing again he said, 'Don't go home with them. I'll drive you if you think your mother will let me stay the night.' To an anxious elder cousin I announced that I was coming home separately, then disappeared; and she, when she got back to the Manor, telephoned my mother and asked, 'Is

Diana home yet? Paul carried her off and I couldn't stop them.' Meanwhile, halted by shut gates at a level crossing, Paul had put his arm round me again and I, my heart thudding, had learnt how to relax and let my head fall against his shoulder. When he turned my face up and kissed me on the mouth, we were both surprised: I because his lips were cold and a little sticky whereas I had expected them to be warm and smooth; he because mine were hot and parted whereas he had expected them to be like a child's. He told me later that he had thought, 'The little devil, she has been at it already, this is not the first time,' but it was. I was thinking, 'Paul is kissing me!'; I was thinking, 'And high time, too'; I was thinking, 'Silly, of course his lips are cold, the night air has been blowing on his face'; I was thinking, 'It is natural for first kisses to be disappointing so it doesn't matter, it will be all right next time.' I was coming into my own at last, as I had always intended to, and the difference between anticipation and reality could only be to the advantage of reality, simply because it *was* reality.

When we arrived at the Farm my mother sat up in bed, furious with worry. 'How could you have behaved like that!' she said. 'Why did you take so long to get home, what did you do?' I meant to say nothing, but I was too full of it to keep it in. 'There was a train shunting at the level crossing,' I said. 'Paul kissed me.'

'Oh,' she said, and I could sense the clutch of fear in her stomach. 'Did he just kiss you, or did he—are you sure he didn't *mess you about?*'

I could not strike her because she was in bed and I was standing some paces away. I could only mutter savagely, 'How could you say that!' and slam out of her room thinking, 'Damn her, damn her, damn her!' I could still feel Paul's dinner jacket against my cheek, those surprising lips, and his hand lightly on my breast where my own hand held it; I was still wrapped about with *the most important moment of my life,* and she had said 'mess you about.'

'They are filthy!' I thought.

Poor parents, what are they to do?

From Christmas 1935 to October 1936 I stayed at home, losing the last shreds of my desire to conform to my family's plan for me by going up to Oxford. I had tried for a scholarship and failed; something of which I was ashamed but which was just becoming a relief when a great-aunt stepped in with an offer to help with my fees. 'Darling Aunt Mary,' they all said. 'How wonderful of her'—and I thought 'Interfering old crone.' Now this is a bad thing to remember: that never, other than formally, did I thank Aunt Mary for the three best years of my life.

I did not know that they were going to be so delightful because I saw them as a continuation of school. Here was I on my eighteenth birthday, and *still* they wanted to stuff education down my throat. But because the months ahead of me, before the first term began, looked so rich and free—a clovery green meadow to a pony who had stood in a stall all winter—I kicked up my heels and forgot about the future. New dresses, friends to stay, dances, reading what I liked, horses, hunting, tennis parties. . . . If I had been asked 'Do you want to do this forever?' I should have answered with an emphatic no, critical as I had become of the structure on which it all rested, and depressing as I found even then the spectacle of girls older than myself who *were* doing it forever—taking the dogs for walks, arranging the flowers, helping their mothers at garden fêtes. No, I did not intend to be like that. But I did want to do it *now*.

Not all of it was pure pleasure. The tennis parties, for instance, almost amounted to misery. My eye sent messages to my hand no more quickly for a tennis ball than for a lacrosse ball; I was always the worst player there and I hated to show at a disadvantage. But they were a large part of our social life as soon as summer began, and that I would not miss. Besides, the white-clad figures against green lawns, the smell of new-mown grass, the taste of iced home-made lemonade, and the presence of men—once the playing was over the parties became enjoyable. Driving to them, I would practise a fierce self-discipline: 'It does not matter if you make a fool of yourself, it does not matter what they think. It is only vanity which makes you think that it matters and if you stop thinking it, it won't.' When this had only depressed me further I would switch to 'And anyway you dance better than they do, and you ride much better, and you read more, and you're a socialist.' It did not do much good, but even so the parties' pleasures were never wholly obscured by their pains.

Hunting had no pains—or rather, its pains were both private and shared, and sharpened its joys. That I was nervous almost to the point of throwing up at every meet, hearing the crack as my horse's forelegs hit the top bar of a gate, the crunch as one of its hooves came down on my skull, was at the same time an internal matter and something in which I was not alone. During the waiting about before the field moves off, many people are likely to be either unusually silent or unnaturally hearty. The more frightened you were, the more miraculous the vanishing of fear as soon as things started to happen; the more exciting the thud of hooves, the creak of leather, the more triumphant your thrusts ahead by risking a blind bit of fence while others were queuing for a straightforward bit. What instinct it is in a horse that gives it its passion for following hounds I do not understand. It is not only the obvious herd instinct, for I have often known horses who continued to quiver and dance, to be alert in every nerve, when we had lost the field and were riding alone, stretching our ears for the hounds' voices, and I once had a pony who was so mad about the sport that she would not eat when she got home after a long day but would lean against the door of her loose-box, straining to hear the intoxicating sounds from which I had had much trouble turning her away several hours before. Whatever it may be, it is shared by the rider, and it is not lust for blood. I used, whenever possible, to avoid being in at the kill, and of all the many people I have known who enjoyed hunting, not one took pleasure in the chase's logical conclusion.

A long hack home after a hard day could be physical torture: cold, stiff, often wet, you could reach a stage when your mount's every stride seemed a jolt, and every jolt drove your spine into the back of your head. That, and the nerves, were part of the game that made it more than a game, that extended you more than you thought you could be extended. At the Manor there would be a groom to take our ponies when we got in, but in Hertfordshire and at the Farm, where we looked after them ourselves, it went without saying that we rubbed them down, fed and watered them and put on their rugs before we plodded our own aching bodies up to their hot baths (oh, the agony of numb fingers coming alive in hot water) followed by tea-with-an-egg. Absurd though one may think the English gentry's obsession with animals, a child gains something from their care. To be able to feel your own chills and fatigues in the body of another creature, to rub them away with a twist of straw and solace them with a bran-mash, is to identify with a being outside yourself.

My family's way of talking about its animals—horses, dogs, and goats—would have sounded absurd to anyone who had no experience of them or liking for them. We saw them not as docile or bad-tempered, ill- or well-trained, but as personalities with attributes similar to those of humans. 'Poor Cinders, he gets so bored in the lower shed,' we might say of a pony; or of a dog, 'Lola is in a very haughty mood.' This anthropomorphic approach to animals, despised by those who do not share it, can be taken to foolish extremes but does not seem to me to be an error. I think Freya Stark put her finger on it when she described the death of a lizard she had once owned. She was grieved to a degree she thought exaggerated until it occurred to her that the distance between the lizard and herself was far less than the distance between her and God, and in that way she expressed a truth which urbanized people forget: that *Homo sapiens* is not a creature apart, but one development of animal life. The more subtly developed animals *do* share with human beings certain muscular movements and actions which express similar states of consciousness; in them these actions are released more directly, by simpler stimuli, but at bottom they are not different and we flatter ourselves if we suppose too great a distance between our own behaviour and that of Pavlov's salivating dog.

I have always taken great pleasure in the company of animals, or even in their neutral presence—a rabbit hopping across a lawn or a bird teasing at some berries in a tree—and I am glad that I was brought up in such a way that this pushing out of feelers into a part of nature other than my own is possible to me. I am also glad that circumstances enabled me to go one step further in this than most of the people among whom I was raised, and ask myself the question 'If I feel like this about dogs and birds and horses—what about those poor foxes?'

It was hares and stags in my case, for ours was not a foxhunting county and we had to make do with harriers and a pack of stag-hounds which hunted deer maintained for the purpose and captured alive after the day's sport, to be returned to their paddock. It was sometimes argued that the older, more experienced deer knew that this was going to happen and fled from the hounds for the fun of the thing, but they did not look as though they thought it fun. I hunted in order to ride. The subtleties of working hounds meant little to me, and throughout my youth the pleasure I got from riding was so great that I averted my eyes and shut my mind to thoughts of the creatures the hounds pursued, but the images registered, all the same. I cannot be certain whether I would have acknowledged them if those months between school and Oxford *had* 'gone on forever' and my country pleasures had continued unbroken, but I believe I might have done. My father did: he did not merely give up shooting, but came to loathe it.

As it happened I was living in London, and no longer killing any-thing, by the time I acknowledged that to kill for amusement was barbaric. Now I detest blood sports. I would never hunt again, nor would I go out to watch anyone shoot, nor even, I think, catch a fish unless I were without food. Living creatures have to prey on each other in order to exist, but not one of them can annihilate another *for its own amusement* without committing an outrage.

For the rest of that time I feel no guilt, though I often behaved badly. Badly in the conventional sense in that I flirted extravagantly with any man willing, considering a dance a failure unless I had been kissed at least once by someone, it did not much matter whom; and badly in another way, in that I became affected and a little arrogant, feeling myself more intelligent than most of my acquaintances, and sometimes (where were those Left Wing principles?) socially superior to some of them. I did not put it like that. At the smaller parties, the local parties, with the sons and daughters of parsons and estate agents and wine merchants and veterinary surgeons, I simply allowed myself to feel that I and my cousins were more dashing and stylish than they were, and showed off accordingly. We could be the stars of those parties (or felt we could be) and I can only hope that the good manners in which we had been trained prevented us from making such monkeys of ourselves as we might have done. If I went to a more sophisticated dance—a dance with people *from London* at it—it was another story. On such an occasion I would be hushed with admiration, and grateful for any attention I received: only if I went to such a dance with Paul could I be quite at ease.

But that exuberant, slightly gauche girl, wearing her hair in a curly fringe because a young man had said that she resembled Katharine Hepburn, does not weigh too much on my conscience. Even if I had never gone to Oxford, I would soon have stopped being eighteen years old.

9

WENT UP TO Oxford in 1936 and I did not join the Communist
Party while I was there. I cannot claim that this was because of
intelligent criticism of Marxist principles, nor that I had an instinctive prescience greater than that of many of my more serious contemporaries: it was simply that I was lazy. Bad smells were as acrid in
my nose as they were in the noses of any other Left Wing undergraduate at the time, and it seemed to me, as it did to others, that only
an extreme, a revolutionary opposition to capitalist society would be
effective. But to become an active Party member—that looked to me
like hard work. As I had slid away from the Church of England, so I
slid away from Communism, but with less excuse: for the first sliding I had felt valid reasons stirring behind the laziness, while for the
second, at that time, I could feel none. I greatly admired anyone who
committed himself and I did not believe that to be, in a desultory
way, a member of the Oxford Labour Club and to cut sandwiches
for hunger marchers was an appropriate response to the circumstances. 'I am,' I felt with regret, 'an essentially frivolous person.'

I felt like that not only when I considered the state of society, but whenever anything forced me to acknowledge that the war would soon be on us. 'We who live in the shadow of a war . . . ' Stephen Spender's poetry I knew by heart several years before I went to Oxford—he had been one of my adolescent passions—and neither he, nor anyone else I read, nor the daily evidence of the news permitted ignorance. But 'Oh shut up, let's talk about something else,' I said. 'There's nothing we can do, anyway.' It was only at night that I would sometimes say to myself the words: 'It is really coming, you know. As things are, it can't fail to come.' One summer night at Oxford there were aeroplanes droning for an hour, circling or streaming over the town for what purpose I do not know. Bombing raids: Spain had given us plenty of book learning about them, but it is odd that I should have known so certainly that the steadily throbbing hum was that of bombers, not fighters. That's how they will sound, I thought, and almost, in the chill of dread, That's them. I cannot remember ever feeling colder or more hopeless when lying in later beds listening to real raids. It was no good pretending that it might not happen: it would. And I cried tears soon dried by their own inadequacy. All I could do about the coming war was to cry. Once I said to a friend, 'I shall kill myself when it starts,' and she replied, 'But that's silly—to kill yourself to avoid death.' It was not death I was thinking of avoiding, it was having to know this horror about life.

So yes: I was frivolous, and I was lazy, and it seems to me now that I was lucky to be those things, because by being able almost all the time to slide sideways, not to think, I could store three years away like jewels before it came.

All the way from home to Oxford I was in a near-coma of alarm, sleepy and detached as though I were watching events from far away and they did not really concern me. Nervousness still has this effect on me, which (though it had unfortunate results during University examinations, making me slapdash and flippant) is a fortunate quirk. Apart from going to school, the only journeys I had ever made alone had been for short visits to friends, for parties, when on arrival I would be met by expected faces and carried off to do expected and pleasurable things. Leaving home frightened me. The super-school for which I supposed myself bound chilled me. I had not believed that those lush green months were going to end so soon.

I had been to Oxford earlier for my interview, so I knew about the gasworks and the marmalade factory and the prison, those melancholy outriders to beauty when you arrive by rail. I knew, too, that my college was an undistinguished building, or sprawl of buildings. If my spirits had been high enough to be dashed, they would not have been dashed by these things. But I did not know quite how institutional my room would be, with its dark-blue curtains of cotton repp, its dark-blue screen round the washstand, its dark-blue cover on the bed and its mud-coloured carpet, limp with use. Oh dear. And then to have to venture out down those long corridors, peer at notice boards, find those other fresh women ('freshers' I would have to call them, I supposed with distaste), all so confident and clever-looking. One had got out of a taxi just in front of me, tall, wearing a fur coat and carrying a bag of golf clubs. Another I had talked to at our interview and she had almond eyes, wore exquisite little shoes, and had dismissed some girl as 'the sort of girl who keeps count of the men who have kissed her'—which I did, too. It was strange that my two best friends should have been the first to catch my attention and to strike awe: Nan, terrified, paralysed with shyness, not knowing what to do with the horrible golf clubs her father had insisted on giving her; Margaret, more like the effect she made but as absorbed by love as I had ever been.

We trooped from interview to interview, being told what we were to do, what classes we were to attend, who was lecturing where, on what; and we were given copies of the Statutes to read. Good God, the restrictions! This would be worse than school. The Statutes have been revised since then, but at that time they appeared to date from my mothers' generation when a girl had to be accompanied by a woman don as chaperone if she went to tea with a man, and naturally no one explained that most of them were ignored.

The first day or two were much as I had feared they would be, though too fully occupied to allow homesickness. It was not until the weekend that the clouds lifted. On the Saturday there was a telegram waiting for me in my pigeonhole: 'FLYING DOWN TO COLLECT YOU TEN O'CLOCK TOMORROW WEAR RIDING CLOTHES PAUL.'

On Sunday I went in to breakfast in riding clothes. The haughty Nan, her fur coat and golf clubs still casting their aura, had kindly kept me a place. Erroneous though my impression of her had been, it was nothing to hers of me when I casually mentioned that my young man was coming to see me *by aeroplane* and that we would spend the morning riding together—it was several days before these two dashing creatures faded away and the real girls met.

Paul had tried to please his father by working for Cadbury's but had not been able to endure it and had bolted into the Royal Air Force after a few months. He was stationed in Lincolnshire but could borrow a plane from time to time and land at Abingdon, where he could borrow a car. I did not much want to ride with him because I despised hired horses and it embarrassed me to see him doing anything at which he was not good—he hardly knew how to ride—but that he should have thought up this way of making me feel at home touched me so deeply that I would have ridden a donkey round Rotten Row all day. And after we had ridden he said, 'I'm going to take you to my favourite place.' We drove to Appleton and there I was, going into the taproom of the Plough for the first time, being introduced to Maggie, who, twenty years later, was to cry 'My God, it's Paul's girl.'

Maggie had a husband, known as Dad, but he was not a very efficient man. It was typical of him that when Paul was staying the night and had to get up at four in the morning to be back in Grantham in time for work, Dad would test the alarm clock to make sure that it was working and would forget to rewind it. He used to smile and nod and be gently shooed into the background by his wife, who ran the place. She looked a little cottage housewife rather than a pubkeeper (in spite of the occasional Guinness hangover), and she gave the impression that opening time was the beginning of a party. Gay, brisk, endlessly generous, she adored an invasion by any of the enterprising young men who had discovered her pub while they were at Oxford, calling them 'her boys'—

and of all 'her boys,' Paul seemed to be the favourite. She would always find a bed for him, lend him money, tell lies for him, scold him, pet him, give him good advice, and welcome his girls without giving any of them a hint that there had been others. She approved of me.

The taproom was narrow and dark, with a solid table down the middle of it and wooden settles along the wall. That was where evenings would begin, or where we would drink when we visited the place at lunchtime. But towards the end of an evening the sheep would divide from the goats—ordinary customers would stay in the taproom, while the more solid 'regulars' and honoured guests would move into the parlour. There was a piano with a pleated silk front in there, and a good deal of shabby furniture in a small space so that we could sit down. It was in the parlour that I spent the first of many Plough evenings, and that I heard the Poacher sing.

Maggie was all for a bit of music and would play herself when she could escape from the taproom. It started, that night, with songs like 'Shenandoah,' or 'When Irish Eyes Are Smiling,' which everyone knew, then went on to the soloists. In the corner sat the Poacher, his cap pulled down over his red face, shuffling his feet and grinning into his mug when people began to urge him. He was coy about it—heaven knows how many pints had to be poured down him before, suddenly, he lurched to his feet. There was a shout of pleasure and he was jostled into the cramped middle of the room. He took off his cap, looked into it for a moment, then slammed it back on to his head the wrong way round. Deliberately, dramatically, he got into his singing posture: one foot advanced, the knee bent, his right arm extended stiffly in front of him (the only other person I have seen in that position was a Maharajah posing for a photograph at the time of King George V's Jubilee). Everyone leant forward in their chairs, and a deep droning sound began, so that I thought 'But what was all the fuss about, the man can't sing at all!' and then I began to hear the words. The Poacher was singing songs composed by the people who had composed the 'Ballads' in my grandfather's wicked white volumes.

'Where did he get them from?' I whispered to Paul.

'From his father. And he got them from his father, and he got them from his. Nobody has ever written them down.'

Back they went into time, the pretty maidens going to market, falling into ditches and showing first their slim ankles, then their round knees, then their white thighs, then . . . A miller went down to his mill to see if his apprentice was filling sacks properly, and found him filling the miller's wife . . . A naïve young shepherdess asked a young shepherd what it was that the rams were doing, and why. . . . Some of them were not lewd but romantic, like the one about a girl lovelorn like a nightingale, leaning her bosom on a cruel thorn. Once the Poacher was launched, others joined in. They all knew the songs and loved them, sentimental or bawdy, and none of them thought of them as anything but 'the old songs' as opposed to 'modern jazz'—none of them thought it strange that they should still be singing them. But when I saw Maggie again after all those years, 'Oh, my dear,' she said to me, 'they never sing the old songs now, not ever. The young ones don't go for them any more and the Poacher's dead.'

I sat through that evening in spellbound silence, made shy by the family greeting Paul got, afraid that I should not be considered worthy. I drank my half-pint of beer to his pint, I watched, I listened, and happiness crept up like a rising tide. Later we drove off somewhere to see a man called Bernard—my first of many a confused exodus at closing time, the cool air of night so sweet on one's face, the handle on the car's door so strangely not quite where one expects it to be, the plans to go to such and such a place changing so mysteriously en route to arrival at another. Bernard was a homosexual, Paul told me as we went up the stairs, but a grand chap, great fun. Goodness, another first! I had never spoken to a homosexual in my life. And soon I was not just speaking to one but was in bed with him, snuggled between him and Paul and drinking whisky, because Bernard it turned out was in bed with a cold and his room was chilly. I was living! Thawed, happy, drunk, kissed, I was delivered back to my college two minutes before midnight when the doors were shut—and I knew that I was going to love Oxford.

To me Oxford became a game at a time when play was life. The play of young animals, their pouncing and stalking and woolly wrestling, is serious. It is learning, without which they would not survive as adults, and that kind of play among human beings is too often restricted by economic necessity to childhood, in which a great deal is learnt, but not everything. Oxford struck me—I am not being wise after the event, it struck me like this at the time—as the perfect place for this kind of learning, or growing. Some of my friends became impatient of it, feeling it unreal, but I argued that if for three or four years you could have the advantages of being adult with none of the responsibilities, what more could you ask? And to have a whole city which, by custom, the young could treat as their own, to be able to walk down its High Street as confidently as though it were your garden path, to be free to be arrogant and absurd—to annoy other people by making loud, precious talk in restaurants, or to carry a grass snake with you when you went to parties—that was the kind of thing which you would never be able to do unselfconsciously anywhere else, and which you needed to do. Behind you were the prison walls of school and the deflating intimacy of family ('No one likes an *affected* girl,' when you had thought you were being witty), and in front of you were the necessary, not unwelcome, disciplines of a job or marriage. But here, now, in the present, was the chance to think and talk and behave in whatever way you wished, and this I could only see as a glorious good.

To say that I did no work while I was up would be to exaggerate only slightly. Certain things I could not avoid: writing an essay for my tutor once a week and attending classes, which were smaller and more intimate than lectures, consisting only of the people from one's own college, in one's own year, who were reading the same subject, visiting some don in his or her room as a group. It was only possible to be absent from a class with a watertight excuse, but no one knew whether one attended lectures or not, since they were a University, not a college, matter, given in the impersonal setting of the University Schools or in the hall of the lecturer's college. I soon thought up the argument that all lecturers wrote books on their subjects, and that one could benefit more from reading than from listening: an argument which would have had something in it if I *had* read, since no form of instruction is more soporific than words spoken to a large audience by someone who has often spoken them before. I must have attended about six lectures in the course of my three years. On those occasions I carried a pen and several sheets of paper, sincerely meaning to take the methodical notes on which, I had so often been told, everything depended. I would get to (3), or perhaps (3a), and then a drawing of a crocodile, a horse, a hat would appear; or a note to show at knee level to Margaret: 'Isn't that man with red hair the one who got drunk at Gerry's party?' 'No, he was fatter.'

I had chosen to read English because I reckoned that I would be reading it anyway, for pleasure. A good deal of it I did read, and wrote about with spirit though always at the last possible moment and too briefly, in essays which gave the impression of intelligence and enthusiasm. But native wit could not disguise for long so thorough a lack of application; indeed, when it came to the barbaric Anglo-Saxon language, an extensive knowledge of which was required, it could not disguise it at all. I was soon starting each term with a little talk from my Moral Tutor—the don responsible for one in a general way throughout one's career. Mine was a small, shy woman of great tact and delicacy of feeling, a scrupulous scholar and a scrupulous respecter of other people's liberties, fastidiously disinclined to bully. Gently, almost humbly, she would ask how I intended to work that term. 'You *ought* to get a First,' she would say during my first year. 'It would be such a pity if you did not.' In my second year it was 'You *ought* to get a Second.' In my third year we reached the point, painfully embarrassing to us both, when she had to steel herself to speak out. 'You cannot do enough work to catch up and avoid disaster if you continue to go out so much, and to act. Rehearsing takes up so much time. I am afraid I really must ask you to think seriously about cutting down your activities—giving up the acting, for instance—now that Schools are nearly on us.'

These interviews made me angry with the itchy, irritable anger which results from knowing yourself to be in the wrong, and after the anger had died down, they made me sorry that I should have inflicted such a disagreeable task on a woman who would so warmly have appreciated the pleasant one of praising me. They did not, however, influence my behaviour in the smallest degree. Even the acting I clung to, although I was no actress and did not think myself one. I only loved everything about it: being onstage, being backstage, making up, painting scenery, the smells, the lights, the sounds.

Intelligent in certain ways I may have been, but I was by nature entirely, hopelessly unscholarly. What I got from Oxford, on the level of formal education (apart from a Third Class degree, and if one were going to do badly the rare Fourth Class would at least have had the merit of dash), was no more than the reading of a few books which I might not otherwise have read and which I am glad to know, and a vague, general idea of what scholarship is. I can recognize it in others, I can wince at its imitations. But if that were all Oxford had given me—or rather, that I had been capable of taking from Oxford—I should have cost my parents and my great-aunt a lot of money for an appallingly small return.

I believe, however, that I owe to Oxford much of the stability and resilience which enabled me, later, to live through twenty years of unhappiness without coming to dislike life. I already had the advantages of a happy childhood and a naturally equable disposition, and three years of almost pure enjoyment added to those advantages confirmed in me a bias towards being *well-disposed* to life without which, lacking faith, lacking intellect, lacking energy, and, eventually, lacking confidence in myself, I might have foundered.

On the river at night, moving silently through the darkness under trees: suddenly the man punting whispers 'Look!' and I turn my head towards the bank. Three naked boys are dancing wildly but without a sound in the moonlight.

On the river at night again, moored in the cave of shadow made by a willow: music in the distance, coming slowly nearer. We stop kissing and another, solitary punter passes us without knowing we are there, with a gramophone in the stern of his punt on which *The Swan of Tuonela* is playing into the night.

In someone's room on an October evening, the air outside the window turning deep blue: a long way away, someone begins to play the Last Post on a bugle and we stop talking while the whole of autumn, the whole of Oxford, the whole of time passing seems to be drawn up into an exquisite sadness. Even at my father's funeral, when the Last Post was played over his grave, it carried me back to that room.

People who have been happy in a first marriage are likely to be happy in a second: they are conditioned to companionship and affection. In the same way, I, having lived for so long in a place which I loved passionately, had a readiness to love another place: it was because of Beckton that Oxford, as a place, meant so much to me. I do not believe that I ever went out of my college, even if only to buy a tube of toothpaste, without taking conscious pleasure in something that I saw, some chime of bells, some smell. Coming back from a class I would deviate from the shortest way to go by the Turl, or by New College Lane or Magpie Lane, or some other street for which I had a particular affection, and I liked to walk by myself so that without distraction I could soak these streets and buildings up. The place seemed to me to give off a physical exhalation to which my very skin responded. If at Oxford anything had irritated, bored, or frustrated me, if I were unhappy or lonely or angry with myself, I could always be restored by the place. Towards the end of my time there I would go out with the deliberate intention of 'soaking up.'

The room which depressed me so much on my first arrival was not mine for long. Soon I was given the chance of moving into better accommodation, and got a room in the Old Building, looking over a lawn with apple trees growing out of neat rounds cut in the grass: 'the unicorn garden' Nan and I used to call it, because it had the look of a garden in a tapestry. My extravagant mother came to visit me and saw at once that all that dark blue, with the ugly washstand, was intolerable. With guilty excitement we hurried out shopping and I chose a shockingly expensive chintz for bed and curtains, and a neat cabinet to enclose the washing paraphernalia which, when shut, looked pretty with a bowl of roses on it. Once books, pictures, and china were arranged, that room became to my mind the most charming and adult-looking in the college, and from that day it was my habit to spend almost my whole allowance of a pound a week on flowers for its decoration. After the detestable promiscuity of school life and the pleasanter but no less unavoidable infringements of privacy in a family, a room of one's own was both an adventure and a reassurance. Thinking it pretty, I even kept it tidy: something which to this day I can only do to rooms I like.

I never used the common rooms except for the short periods during the mornings when I was winkled out of my own by a housemaid; and then, unless it was the morning before I had to produce an essay so that work was unavoidable, I would prefer to visit Nan or Margaret, or to meet friends for coffee in the town. Our social life sounds extraordinarily mild. Except for my escapades with Paul, it was meeting people for coffee, meeting people for a walk, going on the river, going to tea with people—those were by far the most frequent entertainments. There was a scattering of pub-crawls and sherry parties, but few of our young men had more money than we had ourselves, so that although a bottle of reasonably good sherry cost only seven and six, debauchery was usually beyond our means. Except for the summer term, which ended with the Commemoration balls, we were not likely to dance more than two or three times in the eight weeks, while dining at the George, at that time the dashing restaurant, had to be kept for special occasions. Paul took me there, of course, but my undergraduate friends would manage it only during the early, display-dance stage of a wooing.

Because mild though such occupations may sound, they were in fact nearer to being feverish. During nearly all of them love was being approached, made, or dissipated. Sprawling on beds in each other's rooms, Nan, Margaret, and I would certainly often discuss books, politics, religion, and the meaning of life, but more often we would discuss people, and most of the people we discussed were men.

When, and to whom, were we going to lose our virginity? That was our covert, and sometimes our overt, preoccupation. Both Margaret and I had come to Oxford officially in love, and Nan was soon to become engaged, though not for long. Since we all felt that this serious step was synonymous with the sealing of a great love, we should have had no problem—but we did. Not inevitably, but most often, to meet a new man, to be asked out by him, and to get to know him beyond a superficial point was to be embraced by him; and with the embrace he would become at once more than a casual aquaintance, he would become a new person to know. These little explosions of meeting were constantly blasting new shafts into the mine of experience, opening new galleries of relationship to be explored.

Sitting behind two girls in a bus not long ago, I heard one of them saying gravely, 'The trouble is, I'm beginning to think that it *is* possible to be in love with two people at once,' and her words gave me an instant feeling of exhaustion. Yes indeed, that *was* the trouble. How could it not be when the people one was meeting were all different, all real, none of them yet visibly crippled by the patterns their life would impose on them into distrust, or masochism, or boredom, or whatever deformity might overtake them later. I never believed that I would *marry* any of the men I came to know at Oxford—it was Paul whom I was going to marry—but this did not prevent them, sometimes, from being more immediately important to me than mere liking could account for. When Paul was out of sight he was not so much out of mind as tucked away into cold storage in the back of my mind, and during those times other relationships, intense, delightful, or harrowing, could flourish. We all, in the end, steered the course we believed to be right: Margaret married her love soon after leaving Oxford, Nan postponed decision until she was older, and I went to bed with Paul. But it was a serpentine wake that we left behind us before reaching those points, and regularly once a term, I for one would have to spend a day in bed for no other reason than nervous exhaustion.

In one of these subsidiary relationships I was all but trapped, reaching a stage in which I said to myself in so many words 'I love him so much that I would *even marry* him' and clinging to that stage even after I had laughed at my own momentary conception of marriage as a desperate resort. He was the first man I had met for whom I felt the tenderness which comes with physical accord in its purest form: that sympathy between skin and bone and nerves which on its own level is as rare as true temperamental affinity. Simply to look at his thin hands, the way his hair grew crisply above his ears, the slant of his eyelashes and the freckles on the bridge of his nose, gave me such intense pleasure that it *had* to involve the whole of me. I knew perfectly well that although he was a gentle and sweet-natured person, and had a kind of secret integrity of character which was deeply likeable, he was not someone with whom I could communicate. Ideas might flow between me and other people, and between him and other people, but they did not flow between me and him—we came up against a blank wall in each other and a marriage between us would have been a disaster. But we only had to kiss each other for this knowledge to vanish, and at the end of one summer term, when our long, shy love-making had reached a point of tension unbearable to him, we had a scene from which I emerged determined that the first thing I would do at the beginning of next term was to commit myself to him by sleeping with him.

I brewed this decision for the whole of the vacation, becoming more exalted as I became more nervous—and he, at his end, brewed it too, coming, though I did not know it, to an opposite conclusion. He was a level-headed young man with high principles, and he decided that to seduce a girl whom he liked but did not want to marry would be asking for trouble. We met again, I in my fine fever, he in his anxious lucidity—and no other meeting in my life, however much more grave in reality, has remained with me in its detail more painfully than that one. I have written a story about it so I will not describe it here. I will only say that the pain and humiliation and sense of loss seemed to be quite literally unbearable.

So unbearable were they that after two days I saw that I could not bear them. I wrote to Paul: 'Darling Paul,' I said, 'I am so miserable that I want to die. Robert does not love me. Do you think that you can come to Oxford *soon?*'

Back came a letter by return, telling me that even if Robert did not love me, Paul did; telling me that 'he will miss you more than he can bear and will throw care to the winds'; telling me that I must not stop loving or stop being unhappy 'because now you are living';

telling me to 'read Ralph Waldo Emerson in the Oxford Book of E.
V.'; telling me that he was coming.

Before he arrived I did read Ralph Waldo Emerson, a poet whom
I much despised but whose message now, coming through Paul, left
me between crying and laughing:

> *Give all to love;*
> *Obey thy heart;*
> *Friends, kindred, days,*
> *Estate, good fame,*
> *Plans, credit, and the Muse—*
> *Nothing refuse*
>
> *'Tis a brave master;*
> *Let it have scope:*
> *Follow it utterly. . . .*

Oh, darling Paul! What a terrible poem to choose and what a splen-
did message to send! And when I reached the last three lines, miserable though I was, laughter won:

> *Heartily know,*
> *When half-gods go*
> *The gods arrive.*

Whatever Emerson may have intended by that, I had a pretty clear
idea of what Paul meant. 'Oh my love,' I thought, 'what a conceited
old thing you are.'

The comfort that letter gave, the gratitude and affection with which it filled me, were the most adult of all the love-feelings I had yet experienced for Paul. It was at the end of that term that I spent three nights with him in accommodating lodgings which he had discovered when he himself was up at Oxford, and it was during the next vacation that we became engaged.

10

REALITY, AS USUAL, was different from its anticipation. I discovered, for example, that the housework in hotels begins at extraordinary hours. When we spent the week-end of our engagement at Nottingham, which was not far from where Paul was stationed and could be disguised to my family as a week-end in his commanding officer's house, the vacuum cleaners began to hum almost as soon as the washing up of crockery after dinner ended. I had supposed that after making love one always fell into a deep and especially refreshing sleep, and now discovered that one could quite well lie awake all night, limbs twitching under the strain of immobility imposed by fear of disturbing the sleeper beside one. Nor did the earth move under me when we embraced, as Ernest Hemingway had said it would. I knew already that Paul, although an attractive man, was not to me especially attractive—not one of those men like Robert, in response to whose body my every nerve vibrated. Complete love-making confirmed this. It was comfortable and delightful with Paul, but not so totally exciting that my physical sensations became one with my emotional commitment.

I observed these differences from the anticipated, but they did not distress me; they interested me, rather. They interested me constantly and absorbingly in the way that details of life in a foreign country visited for the first time interest me, and I was perfectly confident that I should soon learn my way about them. After a few more week-ends I should be able to turn over and stretch my legs without worrying about Paul's sleep, and after a few more I would find a way to be totally immersed in our love-making. In the short time we were together this did, indeed, begin to happen. He was a gentle and understanding initiator and we knew each other too well for inhibitions or reserves. My confidence was soundly based.

Our families were neither surprised nor displeased when we told them that we intended to marry; only a little anxious, mine because they thought me young for it, his because they knew him to be wild. They all pointed out that to live on four hundred pounds a year, which was apparently what a pilot officer's pay came to in those days, would not be easy, and they all kept telling us that there was plenty of time. I did not see what time was needed *for*. We had agreed that I should not cut short my three years at Oxford—Paul had enjoyed his own time there too much to expect it of me—but that we should be married once my precious last year was over was as certain as the rising of the sun, so why wait before we said so?

I felt selfish in wanting that last year of freedom so much, but it fitted in well. Soon after we had decided to get married, Paul heard that he was to be posted to Egypt at the beginning of that year, and we agreed that it would be a good thing for him to have time to settle down to the kind of work he would be doing there, size up the kind of life we would be living, and find us a house before I joined him. So although I ought not, perhaps, to long so urgently for more people, more emotions, more adventures before I married, I could disguise the longing as common sense.

It is curious now to remember our relationship between my growing up and Paul's departure for Egypt: I would hardly believe in it if I did not still have letters to bear witness. For all that long-short time in my teens I had been the lover waiting to be loved, and for all the long—the really long—time that was to follow, I was to revert to that role, but during this interval, when everything seemed settled, I was confidently, even smugly, the beloved. Paul often told me that he understood my wish to stay on at Oxford and that he wanted me to have my fling, but after these generous gestures he would report nightmares in which he saw me walking away down a street with Robert, and would scribble a miserable note saying 'I know I said I wouldn't mind, but I would, I can't help it.' We would have a wonderful afternoon over at Maggie's, spending hours lying together in the grass by the river, then idling back to the pub for drinks and gossip; and suddenly, rather drunk, I would snap at him with an accusation of possessiveness; or he would press me to decide on the time for a meeting and I would answer coldly that I could not be sure, and I had to see so-and-so, go to a dance with such-and-such. I was not deliberately playing the bitch. I felt that we had a lifetime together—and a lifetime in which Paul would certainly be unfaithful to me whereas I could not see myself being unfaithful to him—so that I still had and deserved time to play

That he would be unfaithful was something that I could not doubt when I knew him so well. For a long time before our engagement he had reported to me on his affairs, filling me at first with awe and with pride that he should choose to confide in me, then with a feeling of security. One of them was 'a very gorgeous and exotic time, but it became indigestible, like an absolute orgy of rich, delicious fruit cake. I can't tell you how wonderful it was to get back to sanity and you.' This was when I was about seventeen, and although I felt a little wry at being considered plain, wholesome fare, I was flattered at being told about it. Later this kind of thing stopped, but even after we had begun to sleep together I had seen him answering a roving eye with an eye no less roving, and I did not believe as firmly as he did in his protestations of absolute fidelity for the rest of our lives. It would be a long time before Paul would be content to leave any situation unexplored.

Once, when we were already engaged, we went out to the Plough in a taxi and since we were both feeling liverish and hung-over, dismissed the cab before we got there so that we would walk the last mile. It was a winter day with a low grey sky above flat brown fields over which fieldfares were flitting. While Paul watched the birds, I watched him. It was soon after I had observed the exchange of roving glances; I was distressed that he should have been ready to click with a girl while I was actually present and he was penitent and extra tender, as he always was when he felt guilty. It will be all right for a long time, I thought. He won't love any of them, he will always come back to me. But I had better face the fact that it will be hell when I get old, when I am *thirty*—and I had a vision of a scraggy neck and pepper-and-salt hair reflected in my mirror. He will still be in his prime then, I thought. That's when I shall have to learn how to be clever, in case he finds love creeping up on him with one of them.

I knew that this problem existed, but it did not worry me deeply. I was sure that I was loved in spite of it, I could see for myself that when I, in my turn, had moments of considering Paul to be plain, wholesome fare, he was more distressed by the role than I was. Perhaps this contributed without my knowing it, to the slightly off-hand manner I slipped into after we were engaged.

Whether that was so or not, the manner had brought him to heel so smartly before a few months were over that it led me into a new development of feeling. Seeing my carefree Paul so distressed, I began to understand that even someone who knew me as well as he did might be confused by my behaviour. If he were to take my love for granted as surely as I did, I must manifest it more clearly, and so I did. The prospect of a year's separation was becoming real; it was easier to sacrifice the small freedoms and the slight independence on which I had been insisting. 'Thank God,' he wrote from the ship, 'that before I left you managed to convince me that you love me as much as I love you. I shall never doubt it again.'

The end of Paul's embarkation leave coincided with the beginning of my term. We had spent a week sailing together at Burnham-on-Crouch, tarnishing my Woolworth's wedding ring in salt water and knowing a more relaxed and lovely intimacy than we had ever had before, and after it I went to London to stay with his family. Our last evening together was wretched. We drank too much and made love unsuccessfully, unhappiness making me cold and stiff, and Paul rough. He cried and I could think of nothing to say to comfort him, nor could I cry myself. The next morning, when he was seeing me off at Paddington, it was I who cried and he who was inarticulate. His parents, my parents, all our friends had been saying 'Never mind, a year is not *really* very long,' and now Paul fell back on this. 'Daddy told me that he waited *four* years for Mummy,' he said through the train window, and I sobbed, 'I don't care. A year is *forever*.' When the train pulled out I thought of going into the lavatory to conceal my tears, but realised that if I indulged in this privacy I should never be able to check them. I stood in the corridor wrestling with them, facing the lavatory door so that the passengers who edged past me should not see my face.

It would have been a horrible farewell if that had been what it was, but in the few days he spent at Grantham before he sailed, Paul gave a typical twist to our parting. He did not warn me but wangled a day off, flew to Abingdon and turned up unexpectedly in Oxford. We clung to each other in the little den of a waiting room in which we had to receive visitors, and knew that everything had become smooth and natural again: the good-byes were done with, we could be together. We went to Maggie's and were happy all that day, and when he left it was almost as though there were nothing special about our parting. A year had become just a year. In Egypt I was going to ride a white Arab stallion and keep a white saluki to run behind me. We were going to have four children—Paul had always wanted children on the grounds that creation, in whatever form, was the justification of living, so that for people like ourselves, who could not write or paint or compose, children were the thing. I had as yet no stirrings of maternal feeling, but was prepared to believe that I would like babies once they were there. 'I expect you will change your mind and come out to me sooner than you think,' said Paul, and I answered, 'I expect I shall.'

So Oxford became a good place to wait in. Flaking stone, blue mists over the river, laburnums showering over garden walls in the road leading to my college, the scent of stocks and roses from behind the walls, voices calling up to windows, and the charming frivolities of friendship now suddenly revealing a deeper value than I had suspected. Even love still went on, though now that I was committed to Paul it was different. Once the obsessing question of virginity had been solved, the clouds of sex rolled back a little and I became more familiar with affection, patience, tenderness, and understanding, all of which I accepted gratefully, even greedily, as something to keep me warm while I waited for Paul's letters. Perhaps, at that time, I enjoyed Oxford even more intensely, knowing that my 'real' life was already being lived for me—half of it, at any rate—in Egypt.

I was both nervous and arrogant at the prospect of becoming an 'RAF wife.' The other wives, I was sure, would talk of nothing but their servants and would play bridge every afternoon. I would have to be a rebellious and eccentric wife, I decided, and Paul's letters suggested that this could be achieved fairly easily. It was true that he reported that no one else on the station met Egyptians or ate Egyptian food—'They might be Colonel Blimp in person, every one of them,' he said—but he himself had made the rounds of the Arab night clubs in Cairo before he had been there a week, enjoyed the food and was guest of honour at an Arab village wedding within three weeks. He wrote about Egypt with a lively tourist's relish, easily tickled by the picturesque or the comic: not a particularly serious or understanding approach, but an open, welcoming one. He described the problems of sailing a dhow; the white Arab stallion was going to materialize—a man in the neighbouring village knew of a perfect one; we would ride far into the desert, we would sleep out, we would meet nomads. It seemed likely that by the time I arrived his 'Arab technique' would be almost as good as his 'pub technique.'

The RAF wives, he said, were not so bad as I had expected and would be kind and helpful, but we would have more fun than they did: not for us the narrow circle of club, swimming pool, and bridge table.

He worked out a budget for us—something which neither of us had ever done—proving that we could live on £24 a month, with a furnished house, a servant, a car, and plenty to drink ('Mind you, we could live cheaper than £24 a month, but it would be more fun if we didn't'). 'Our gloomy pictures of marital boredom are quite impossible,' he wrote. 'My day and your day—an ordinary day, when we weren't doing anything special—would be like this: 5 a.m.: I get up and go to the camp in car to work. 7.30 a.m.: I return for breakfast, by which time you have got up and quite probably will have already been for a ride with the saluki on your white Arab. 8.30 a.m. to 12.30 p.m.: I work and fly. You drive into Cairo, do some shopping, bathe at the Ghezira sporting club and have some lovely-looking Frenchman flattering you. 12.30 p.m.: Both home to lunch. 1.30 p.m. to 5.30 p.m.: The whole of Egypt sleeps in a temperature of about 105 in the shade, but a lovely, dry, energizing heat!!!! 5.30 p.m. to 6.30 p.m.: Tea and toast and baths and wanderings about in kimonos. 7.00 p.m.: Drinks and friends. 8.30 p.m.: Cairo for dinner, dancing, and cabaret. 2.00 a.m.: Bed.' Mentally turning half of the shopping time into reading time, I had to acknowledge that this deplorably idle life, provided it were lived with Paul, would be just the life for me.

I always knew when Paul's letters had come. Before I had opened my eyes in the morning, something in me would have sniffed the air and I would know. He wrote well, and at length, but not often, so that morning after morning lassitude would come over me again and I would have to struggle not to bury my face in the pillow and go back to sleep. Then a morning would come when I would be out of bed without thinking of it. I would try to dress slowly and calmly, and not to run downstairs, telling myself not to be excited in case I was wrong, but I was never wrong.

When Hitler invaded Czechoslovakia I knew that I had been a fool. We only had time to draw a deep breath before the war began, so I wrote to Paul telling him that I had indeed changed my mind and was ready to join him at once. He answered with delight, but hardly had his letter arrived than it was followed by a cable saying that he had been transferred to Transjordan, then in a state of emergency, and that we must revert to our plan of marrying at the end of the year. He was transferred. I had two more long, alive, loving letters from him, and then I never heard from him again until I received a formal note, two years later, asking me to release him from our engagement because he was about to marry someone else.

11

THE TIMES WHEN the pain was nearest to the physical—
to that of a finger crushed in a door, or a tooth under a
drill—were not those in which I thought 'He no longer
loves me' but those in which I thought 'He will not even write to
tell me that he no longer loves me.' For weeks his silence seemed
no more than his usual unreadiness as a letter writer; then, for
months, the result of his absorption in his work and in the place
where he was working, both of which he had described with vibrating enthusiasm. Such excuses I went on making for much longer
than any detached observer could have accepted them, shutting my
eyes in panic to the considerate silences and distressed expressions
of my mother and my friends. I remembered what he had said in
the third but last letter I had from him: 'Never write to me less
often. I know that I don't deserve it, but it is terribly hard to write
here and I'm bad at it anyway, so if you don't hear from me often
enough you must never think it's because I am not thinking about
you. I think about you *all the time* and I would die if you stopped
writing to me.' So I went on writing, and I tried not to complain

at getting no answers. But after a while my letters became involuntarily appealing, then humiliatingly pleading, then unconvincingly threatening. Before I myself became silent—after how long I cannot remember—I had thrown off all attempts at consideration, strategy, or pride: I had told him as nakedly as I could what his silence was doing to me—and still it continued.

If he had written to say, 'For such and such a reason I no longer want to marry you, I no longer love you,' I should have been stunned with grief and loss but it would have made some kind of sense and I could have come to terms with it. But that Paul, who had loved me, and who knew what I was now feeling, should have wiped out my existence so totally . . . I was often literally unable to believe it, it was something he *could not* do.

It was not until many years later that I learnt the reason for what had happened—a love affair, of course, although not with the girl he was to marry. Feelings of guilt snowball. When they have accumulated beyond a certain point, a sense that nothing can annul them makes any action seem inadequate, so that oblivion becomes the only easy answer. Paul, who was never good at doing anything which he disliked, must have felt at first that a time would come when he would be able to explain, then that the time had taken too long in coming. So he cheated; he shut his imagination.

If I had known him less well the whole thing might have been over comparatively quickly: I might have written him off as a monster, dropped all hope, and have been cured. Two things prevented this. One was the reaction common to almost everyone in such a situation: the terrible knowledge that if you accept the unworthiness of the object of your love, then your love itself is discredited and all the good in its past becomes poisoned retroactively. The other was the plain fact that Paul was not a monster. I had known him for so many of the longest years in a life-time, I had grown up with him, I had loved him, after the first spell of childish infatuation, with the sort of love which brings knowledge rather than illusion: I was unable to make a grotesque of him. He was a spoilt young man who lived intensely in the present, and I had always known that in whatever place he happened to be, his present would be there. It was not in his nature to live suspended between past and future, as I could do. So although there were many times when I was cornered by that worst of all manifestations of suffering—the certainty that what is happening, what is being done, is too painful to be borne, but that the logical consequence of this, which would be that therefore one would not have to bear it, is simply not going to come about—although this happened night after night, and although I laboured through long stretches of incredulity and anger, and great bogs of self-pity, I always came back to the knowledge that it was not Paul's fault that our relationship had become unreal to him.

Knowing this, I would not give him up. When he came back to England, I was sure, I would again become his present. At one point, about eighteen months after he had fallen silent, a cousin told me that a man she knew had met Paul at a drunken party, somewhere in Palestine, and that when Paul had learnt that this man knew Beckton, my family, and me, though only slightly, he had burst into tears (he always cried easily when thoroughly drunk). He had wept, he had said that he was a worthless brute, he had said that I was the only woman he really loved. My cousin, it seems to me, took a risk in passing on this report to me, because it might have led me to build some wild structure of hope, but in fact it did no harm because the structure was already there. I simply took it as confirmation of what I already believed: if Paul and I were to meet again—I could see that in all probability we would not, but if we did—it would be possible to overcome what had happened. More than any other image of him, I remembered a moment when, in a room full of people, he had come across to light my cigarette, our eyes had met, I had felt my own changing and I had seen his lighten from brown to gold as the flash of understanding passed between us. Whatever happened in the interval, I was convinced that if we saw each other again a moment would come when our eyes would do that; that while I remained myself and Paul was Paul, we could not be together without being as we had been.

Perhaps this might have happened if the war had not prevented his return to England. He was then cut off from us, and flying bombers, with the airman's usual cold knowledge of the chances against his ever coming home again. England and everything in it must soon have become incredibly remote to him, and who knows what chill stretches of loneliness he must have lived through, loving his lost home and his lost life as he did, before he met a girl who could give him warmth and certainty, and whom he married. He was killed before their son was born, but at least he knew that they were to have a child. It is now easy to be grateful to that girl for having existed (she married again, I am happy to say), but at the time. . . .

His final letter, arriving after two years had passed, with its formal request 'to be released' from our engagement, seemed to me so cruel that I still cannot think of it as having been written by Paul. It seemed cruel not because of its contents but because of its wording. It was written in the kind of words men use in letters to women who, unless everything is 'cleared up,' might sue them for breach of promise, and that Paul should write in that way to *me* seemed to annihilate the half of our years together that had existed in his mind. The manner was dictated, I can now see, by guilt and embarrassment. It would have been no more possible for Paul to remember me as such a woman than it would have been for me to remember him as mean or vindictive. But when the letter was brought up to me early one morning by my silent mother, my body went cold and limp on the bed at the image it suggested of what I had become in Paul's memory. Then I dropped the horrible piece of paper and thought, Well, anyway, it's over now. The final desolation was to see, even as I thought the words, that it was not. The picture which came into my mind was of a long bridge suspended between two towers. One of the towers was knocked away, so surely the bridge must fall—but it did not. Senselessly, absurdly, it went on extending into space.

The humiliations of grief are revolting. If only I had kept silent! But in the short letter I wrote back I permitted myself the whining, miserable words 'I hope you never make her as unhappy as you have made me' and I have never been more ashamed of anything I have done. That was the kind of thing about being unhappy which I loathed: the spectacle of oneself being turned into something despicable. That was what I struggled against, and for that reason I was pleased for many years by the knowledge that I had never for any length of time lost my hold on the truth of the situation: never, at bottom, held Paul 'guilty' for what had happened. But now I am not sure that this was so fortunate.

Paul was not any 'guiltier' than any other human being—all are capable of the unpardonable from time to time—but if I had let myself feel that he was, I believe the effects of his desertion might have been less far-reaching. By heaping blame on to him, I might have kept my confidence in myself intact. As it was, frightened by a vision of myself gone sour and self-pitying, I went further than allowing the situation not to be his fault—I took 'fault' on myself. 'Why should he have gone on loving me in absence?' I began asking myself bleakly. 'The fact that he was not able to do so proves that I am not the sort of person who has the right to expect such a thing.' During the nights which followed the blank, heavy days, when bitterness began to mount in me, I would hammer it down with this thought.

A long, flat unhappiness of that sort drains one, substitutes for blood some thin, acid fluid with a disagreeable smell. When in those days I stared at myself in the looking glass it seemed to me that I was the same as usual: my colour normal, enough flesh on my bones, my hair shiny. But I had proof that I was not the same. People had noticed me when I was happy, had chosen my company, and laughed with me and tried to make love to me. When I was no longer happy they did none of these things, they saw something about me which made them avoid me. I remember telling myself that this was subjective, that it was I who was not responding to other people—none of them had any quality other than being not-Paul—so the lack of contact came from me, not them: self-pity, I told myself, was working on my imagination. Before I went to a party I would try to persuade myself that if I expected to enjoy it I would do so, and then there would be no more of those eyes straying in search of other glances while flat talk was made. No one, I would assure myself, was thinking of me as diseased—why *should* anyone think of me in that way? But the most horrible moment of that horrible time was not imagined.

One of our family friends was an exceptionally attractive, slightly raffish man, nearer my parents' generation than my own, with whom I might well have fallen in love if I had not been otherwise occupied. He was just the man for it: tall, lean, very handsome in a fine-drawn way, he had bummed romantically about the world busting broncos, sailing on tramp steamers, ruining his health (who knew how?) in places full of parrots and mangrove swamps. My own acknowledgment of his charms remained detached, but not so that of my sister. She, five years younger than I was, felt his glamour to the point of hero worship, and he, tickled by this and observing that an attractive child was developing into a lovely girl, used to flirt with her. She was a busy diarist, filling fat notebooks by the dozen, writing 'Secret' on them and leaving them about in her bedroom so that her private life was not so private as she hoped. I am sure that my mother read those diaries from end to end, and I too would leaf through them from time to time, half amused, half sympathetic. My sister's passion for this man was faithfully recorded, and so was his mischievous but harmless response to it.

Once, driving her back from some party, he held her hand. When they got home they sat for some minutes in the car and she, dizzy with expectation, thought that he would kiss her. He did not. 'He told me that he was not going to kiss me although he wanted to. He said that I was going to be a fascinating woman but that I mustn't begin that sort of thing too soon or it would spoil me. *Look at Di, he said, you don't want to be like her. And of course I don't.*'

The shrivelling sensation of reading those words is something I still flinch from recalling. I could not even summon up indignation at their smugness and unfairness, or question the misconception that 'being like Di' resulted from being loved too soon instead of from misery at being loved no longer. With a shameful, accepting humility I saw that I *was* diseased in other people's eyes: that unhappiness was not a misfortune but a taint. In the depths of my being I must have wanted to kill my sister for it, but all I recognized was a shuddering acknowledgment that out of the mouths of babes. . . . Pretty and vital as she was, for many years after that I saw her as prettier and more vital, and was prepared to take second place to her, to rejoice at her triumphs and fret over her sorrows like a model sister. This was not a bad thing, since she gave good reason for admiration and affection, but there was a streak of falsity in it: I was overcompensating for my resentment at the scar she had left with her innocent, idle thrust.

Some time after that, during the first May of the war, I was invited for a week's sailing on the Broads. There would be six of us: Hugh, the young doctor who had asked me, who would be paired with a pretty cousin; an engaged couple, both of whom I liked; and a friend of Hugh's to pair with me. The girls were to sleep on the boat, the men ashore, in tents. Every week that the war continued 'phony' was, we knew, a week to grab. It had not yet closed the Broads for defence purposes, but it had driven people off them, so that we would see them as they are never ordinarily seen, free of motor launches, houseboats, and picnickers. The weather was miraculous, a springtime out of a pastoral poem, and I felt a lift of heart at being invited. Sailing I loved, and Hugh must want me with them or he would not have asked me. Perhaps I would be able to enjoy something, at last, enough to break through the barrier and get a foot back into life.

Two days before we were to start, Hugh telephoned to say that the man invited for me had failed us, his leave had been cancelled. It would make it less amusing for me, they feared, but please would I come all the same, it was not the kind of party on which even numbers mattered. I felt foreboding, but I went.

During most of each day it was true, even numbers did not matter. We were busy sailing and sunning and preparing absurd meals, all enjoying having those strange waterways to ourselves, manœuvring through the narrow cuts, coming quietly out on to the wide expanses with nothing on them but coot, grebe, and duck. No people. We seemed to have gone back in time to a wild, untouched country. Both Hugh and the engaged ones knew of Paul's long silence and were kind and welcoming, doing their best to include me and to cheer me up. But the engaged ones *were* engaged—and the little girl cousin was fiercely in love with Hugh. She had no reason to be jealous of his amiability to me, but she was; and he, although not deeply involved, was touched by her; he could not do anything but treat her, gently, as his love. When the early evenings fell, when we had wrestled with our primus stove and eaten, and the moon had sailed up above the rushes, it was inevitable that the two couples should link up.

The engaged ones would take the dinghy and paddle off, leaving an uneven wake of silvered ripples on the smooth, inky water. Hugh, the girl, and I would wash up, sit on the deck to talk in low voices, and the tension would mount. It was painfully beautiful. Reed warblers (Paul would have known if they were really reed

141

warblers) would toss off little beads of song, almost like nightingales, and the uncanny booming of the bitterns—more like some ancient monster bellowing—sent shivers down my spine. After a while the couple's wish to be alone would force me to my feet. 'I know what *I* want to do,' I would say, my wretched humility brightening my voice. 'I'm going for a walk to see if I can get nearer to that bittern.' Hugh would go through the motions of asking the girl whether she wanted to go too, and she would go through the motions of deciding that no, on the whole she thought she was too sleepy.

I did not cry as I wandered by myself through the tufty marsh grass. I tried to be only my senses, soaking outwards into the beauty, savouring night-time, of which one always has too little—and I must have succeeded up to a point because when I remember that week the beauty is still sharply with me. But only a yogi could keep that up, and I had to face the truth. This was before I had heard of Paul's marriage, but far enough on for my belief in his return to have been reduced to its minimum: less a belief in his return, than a belief that *if* he returned, all might be well. On the night when the moon was full I had to put aside that belief. On that night there was no cloud in the sky, but there was a wind. It came rushing between the moon and the flat land, bending the forest of reeds where earth melted into water with such a steady, even thrust that it hardly made them rustle. With the same relentless flow it seemed to flood through my emptiness. Out on the Broad the engaged couple would be whispering and laughing; in the boat's cabin Hugh and the girl would be holding each other close and kissing. I stood under that moon, in that wind, and knew myself to be absolutely alone. It was so absolute that for a time I might have been my skeleton lying somewhere, as Paul's was soon to lie, to be picked clean by the elements.

It was a feeling far too powerful to be evaded; it had to be accepted. 'This is it,' I thought. 'This is how it is,' and with a sort of dull, weary recognition I saw that it could be endured, and that if *that* could be endured, then anything could be. After about an hour I went back to the boat to find that the others had reassembled as a party and were brewing tea. Hugh reached out and squeezed my hand in the cabin's almost-darkness, for which I am still grateful to him. And from that time I made better progress in my discipline against self-pity and it was less bad than it had been, or so I thought. But perhaps it was that experience of absolute acceptance which put the seal on my loneliness for so much of my life.

To be in love and engaged at nineteen, and disengaged at twenty-two, is not fatal: you have lost your love, you have lost your job (for that is what it amounts to for a woman, as surely as though she had been training to be a doctor, only to be prevented by circumstances from practising), but you are still very young. 'You are still very young,' I used to tell myself. 'It is absurd to consider your life ruined at this age. However improbable it may seem, someone else will take Paul's place.' And that, naturally, happened. What my self-admonishment did not take into account was the change brought about in my nature by my own loss of confidence.

Why should my sense of my own value in relationships with men have collapsed so completely? I have sometimes wondered whether the smallness of the part played by my father in my childhood may have been responsible. Did I once, long before I can remember, want to fall in love with him as little girls are supposed to do, and was I chilled by an indifference that left me with a tendency to expect rejection? It would make sense, it is the sort of explanation offered by convincing textbooks, but it seems a bit too simple to me.

Whatever the reason for it, there was a flaw of some sort in me which split under the impact of my abandonment by Paul and ran through all my subsequent relationships with men until I believed that I had come to the end of them. Love still took up most of my attention, but to describe in any detail my other affairs would be tedious, because they ran to a pattern. I could only be at ease in a relationship which I knew to be trivial. If I fell seriously in love it was with a fatalistic expectation of disaster, and disaster followed. By the time I had reached my thirties I was convinced that I lacked some vital quality necessary to inspire love, and it was not until my forties were approaching that I began to see the possibility that instead of lacking it, I might have been suppressing it; that my profound 'misfortune,' of being unable to make the men I loved love me in return, might be the result of an attitude of my own which came from a subconscious equating of love with pain.

Twice I fell in love with happily married men—the first time quite soon after Paul's marriage. It felt like coming back to life with a vengeance, but I recognized from the beginning that it was 'hopeless,' in that when he said 'love' he meant something less than I did, and the more I recognized this, the greater my secret abandon to the situation. It must have been chance that he repeated the pattern of Paul so exactly—going away, writing a few times, then silence—but although this second blow on the same spot was an agony, it was not *unexpected:* I had been waiting for it from the moment I realized that this was a 'real' man, not just a man who was not Paul. And both with that man and with my second married lover, I flattered myself that I was unselfish and fair-minded in not wanting to force them into leaving their wives: indeed, their affection for their wives, underlying their readiness to enjoy themselves with me, was something which I esteemed. I felt with both of them that they would not have been the kind of man I could have loved so much if they had been prepared to wreck long-standing marriages for my sake, and estimable though this attitude may be on the face of it, there now seems to me something fishy about it. I was hungry to be alive, so I was hungry to love—but was I hungry, in fact, for the companionship of those particular men, or of the third one, unmarried but not in love with me, whose reservations about me turned a lively attraction into infatuation so that I did not *fall* in love with him, but might have been *jumping* off a cliff? I have always shrunk from the idea of possessiveness, I have never tried to mould people into my own idea of them, and I have been satisfied with myself because of this; I have considered it a virtue. It may have been in part the virtue I took it to be, but I suspect now that it had other aspects as well: that if I did not grab at people, I grabbed at emotion, and that for many years the most intense emotion I could conceive of was one of pain.

12

'OF COURSE IT'S different for someone like you, a career woman. . . .'

Good God! I thought, and was about to protest. But what is a woman with a job and no husband, once past thirty, if not a career woman? I remembered a book in a blue binding which, when I was twelve, I shared with my friend Betty: a book with questions in it, and spaces for the answers. Who is your favourite character in fiction? What is your favourite food? What is your ambition? Betty wrote that her ambition was to be a great actress. Mine was: 'To marry a man I love and who loves me.' I never went back on that and I do not go back on it now, but I have not made it; so a career woman is what I look like, and what do I think of *that*?

At Oxford and immediately after I left it, I was extremely naïve about careers. So was the rest of my family. It is astonishing to remember how few working women we knew—none at all well, except for my mother's unmarried sister, who had been a hospital almoner until she was arbitrarily summoned home to live with my grandmother on my grandfather's death. Sometimes a report would come in that so-and-so's daughter—'such a clever girl'—had got 'a wonderful job in the Foreign Office' or was 'doing so well on the *Manchester Guardian.*' We would admire this, but the mere fact that the girl was in such a job removed her from our sphere and made her seem a different kind of person from oneself. I never had any doubt that the kind of job I would like would be one connected with literature, painting, or the theatre, but that sort of thing seemed far outside my range. I had a humble idea of my own abilities. I lacked the proper arrogance of youth in that respect. Lazy and self-indulgent, I was a lively girl only in my capacity as a female, and once I was wounded in that capacity I became, to face the truth, dull. (Since I believe that any recognition of truth is salutary, this should be a bracing moment, but it does not feel like that: it feels sad.)

So instead of having some wild but inspiriting ambition I thought vaguely that I might like to be a journalist because I enjoyed writing letters and essays, or I might like to be a librarian because I enjoyed reading books. I did not have to read many newspapers before I saw that I was probably off-beam about the first, so the second was what, in a half-hearted way, I was planning to be when the war began.

The war began. I sat on the dining-room floor at the Farm with my sister, filling bags of hessian with fine, prickly chaff to make mattresses for refugees from London, while we listened to Chamberlain's announcement on the radio and swallowed our tears. (I do not remember that any of the refugees actually slept on those emergency mattresses, but most of them stampeded back to London quite as fast as if they had.)

I was no longer a pacifist in any formal sense. To make gestures against the war once it had come seemed as absurd as to make gestures against an earthquake or a hurricane. The horror had materialized and it must be endured, but to *participate* in it any further than I was compelled to do by *force majeure* did not occur to me. A mute, mulish loathing of the whole monstrous lunacy was what I felt; almost an indifference to how it ended, for no matter who won the war, it had happened; human beings—and I did not recognize much difference between German human beings and English ones—had proved capable of making it happen, and that fact could never be undone. Later, when 'unconditional surrender' was the watchword and furtive peace feelers from the Axis were being snubbed, the madness seemed to me to have become so great that my imagination could not even *try* to comprehend it.

To have become a nurse would have made sense to me, but I knew in my bones that I had no gift for nursing. To have joined one of the women's services was something that I could have done, becoming one of thousands of regimented women, learning to talk military jargon, growing ruddy under a uniform cap and broad-beamed in khaki bloomers. It seemed to me an intensely disagreeable prospect, but what particular right had *I* to avoid it? I cannot remember even attempting to think of a justification. I was determined that I would not do it unless 'they' came and got me, and that was that.

This refusal to take any part not forced on me seems to me now an unmistakable measure of smallness of spirit. To remain detached from the history of one's time, however insane its course, is fruitless even on the private level, since only by living what is happening (whether by joining it or by actively opposing it) can the individual apprehend its truth. Detestable as the 'white feather' mood of the First World War certainly must have been, an expression of all that was most ridiculous in 'patriotism' and most hysterical in suffering ('My man is going to be killed so why shouldn't you be killed too?'), it had in it a grain of truth: there can be no separateness from the guilt of belonging to the human species—not unless the individual withdraws into a complete vacuum and disclaims participation in the glories as well. There are two honest courses when war strikes: either to make some futile but positive gesture against it and suffer the consequences, or to live it—not in acceptance of its values, but in acceptance of the realities of the human condition. I did neither, and I have no doubt that I was wrong. 'Living' the war, for me, would have amounted to no more than putting on uniform and working, most probably, at some kind of clerical job for the purpose of 'releasing' a man so that he could kill and be killed. It would have been as stupid a thing to do as I felt it to be at the time, but by handing over my freedom in that way I would have tasted *what was happening,* which is the duty of anyone who wants to understand, to be aware, to touch the truth. It could be argued that the civilian jobs in which I ended up served the same purpose as a job in the services would have done, since I would not have been allowed to remain in those jobs if the officials responsible for directing my labours had not classified them as 'essential.' The difference was a subjective one. I chose civilian work because it represented the minimum loss of personal freedom possible in the circumstances, and loss of personal freedom was exactly the phenomenon most characteristic of the situation I should have been exploring. It was the people in concentration camps who were drinking most deeply the poison of what was happening; they, and men like the soldiers from West Africa and the Sudan, carried on the tide of madness into a war that could mean even less to them than it did to me. The actual consequences of any choice of mine were, of course, too infinitesimal to be perceptible outside my own skull; but within my skull, the choice I made was of a kind to build a wall between such people and myself.

It follows, naturally, that one should be to some extent 'engaged' at all times, not only in times of crisis: that I am no less wrong now than I was then, since I still take no part in any sort of political or social activity; I have never marched against the hydrogen bomb, I have never distributed leaflets urging the boycotting of South African goods. Whether, believing this, I shall some day turn to action, I do not know: given my record, it seems unlikely. Both by conditioning and by instinct I continue to cling to the wrappings of self-indulgence which keep safe my privacy and my female sense of another kind of truth running beside the social one: the body's truth of birth, coupling, death that can only be touched in personal relationships, and in contemplation.

Determined not to join the services, I answered an advertisement for women to build small boats in a factory at Southampton, supposing that because the boats were small the factory would be small too. I imagined it with a boatyard attached to it in which, though I might not be permitted to build a whole boat single-handed, I would work on recognizable features of boats—shape a tiller, perhaps, or screw cleats into place. The papers I received indicated that I was mistaken. Engagingly, one of them was a form on which I was to state whether I preferred my dungarees to be sky blue, apple green, or rose pink, but the rest of it gave a clear picture of monotonous hours doing something with metal at a factory bench. To anyone as spoilt as I was, the working day seemed atrociously long, and the wages made me sceptical forever of sweeping talk about big money earned by factory hands. Such talk was in the air—'Those are the people who have the money, of course'—but the factory which might have been mine paid a disconcertingly small basic wage and only someone made of steel could have earned overtime. Because I could hardly back down at that stage, I said that I would wear sky-blue overalls and waited for instructions, but my relief was great when I received an apologetic letter saying that they had no more vacancies after all.

Then I heard from a friend that the Admiralty, removed from London to Bath, was recruiting women busily. My enquiry was answered by a kind, discouraging letter asking why I wanted an ill-paid office girl's job when there were surely other things I could do, but I persisted. I did not want my refuge to be comfortable. To be bored, badly paid, but useful seemed to be what the situation required.

Bored I would have been, had it not been for Bath and the friends I made there; badly paid I was, pocketing fifteen shillings and ninepence a week after the money for my billet had been deducted; useful I was not. The permanent civil servants, uncomfortably over-worked in requisitioned hotels and schools, had little time to teach undisciplined recruits, however willing. They were burdened not only by me, but by a large number of young men and women from the neighbourhood who saw working for them as a good way of filling in time before they were called up (if men) or could persuade their parents to let them go further afield (if women—labour was still undirected at that time). I was so conscious of my own ineffi-ciency that I would have accepted brusque treatment as just, but the regulars were charmingly kind and patient. They gave me and my like documents marked 'SECRET' to carry from one room to another, they let us make tea (although we made it too weak), and they sat us down to use logarithm tables at which they supposed, mistakenly, no one could go wrong. In the end my harassed master used to give me a sheet of paper and say, 'Copy this on to that.' I would copy it carefully, he would say, 'Good, thank you very much,'—but once I saw him slip my copy into the waste-paper basket.

I felt at first as though I were in an uneasy but not intolerable dream. The close ranks of inky desks in the dining-room of the Pulteney Hotel, the stacks of forms referred to by numbers and initials, the scratching nibs, the tin trays marked 'PENDING'—all this made sense to the others, obviously, but not to me. I knew that my sub-section of a sub-section of a department was concerned with transferring equipment for mine-sweepers from one naval base to another, but I could not envisage the equipment and no one seemed to know anything about it either before or after its transfer. Gravely and carefully, these rather tired middle-aged men laboured away at their ant-like task, and in the years they had spent on such things they had built up a small, snug office world with its own rites, necessities, taboos, and humours: not by any means a disagreeable world, not a world one could dislike or despise when one saw it at close quarters, but not a world to which I could imagine myself belonging. I would leave it each evening and return to a little box of a bedroom in a council house owned by a platelayer. His wife would give me a sturdy supper, and then I would lie on my bed and read. After Beckton and Oxford, this was too *odd* to be depressing. I simply felt suspended, waiting dumbly to see if I would ever begin to find my bearings.

Soon my voice was noticed by a snobbish but helpful woman who had volunteered to drive for the Admiralty and ferried people to work from the remote suburb in which I was staying. Would I not like, she asked, to be transferred to more congenial billets? I had not supposed such a move to be possible, tried to suppress a start of hope (because the platelayer's wife, though reserved, was a kind landlady), and mumbled that if it could be done. . . . To my surprise she remembered to speak to the billeting office, and I was whisked into the town to be established with a family of Christian Scientists so astonishingly generous and welcoming that I have had a weakness for the sect ever since. In their benevolent, easygoing flat I could wake up.

Every day I walked to the office across the Royal Crescent, through the Circus, down Gay Street—oh, lovely Bath! There is no city in England more beautiful than that one, stepping down into its bowl of mist. There was always something to look at—a fanlight, a wrought-iron cage for a lantern, a magnolia growing out of a basement against the soot-dimmed golden grey of stone—but my chief daily joy was the great arc of the Crescent, with its broad, worn paving stones, its spacious view, and the curious silence it holds within its curve. A man who was walking me home one night said, 'It's like going into a church,' and I was speechless for several minutes in outrage at hearing my own feelings put into such clumsy words.

Before long I had become flippant about the job and had made one of the most charming of all my women friends. She emerged like a dragonfly from the dull envelope of a letter of introduction: 'Your dear Aunt tells me . . . We would be so pleased if you would come to tea on Sunday.' The youngest daughter of a spirited Irish family, polite but unenthusiastic, was sent to fetch me, and within an hour I had tapped a source of amusement and drama on which I can still, today, rely. Where Anne goes, disaster strikes: disaster too extreme for anything but laughter. If we borrowed her father's car without asking him, it was stolen; if we went to London for a night to meet young men, we lost either our tickets or the keys of our baggage, and our dresses split as we put them on; if we had no money but one penny and one half-crown, it was the half-crown we dropped into the slot on a lavatory door. 'Imagine what's happened *now*,' Anne would say (and still says), and out would come a vivid, exaggerated story of the bizarre, the macabre, or the absurd. I have always liked to watch pretty women and have enjoyed the company of gay ones: she, one of the prettiest and gayest I know, as well as one of the most generous, courageous, and, at times, infuriatingly perverse, became and remained a friend to be thankful for.

Living a new kind of life away from home, where I had been my unhappiest more recently than my happiest, I was often at that time able to dodge my misery over Paul. Laughter, frivolity, even silliness and affectation (and Anne and I must often have been silly and affected) are dependable salves in my experience, besides being strong threads in feminine friendships. I enjoyed much of my time at Bath and was sad when I decided that I had better resign before I was sacked, and go home to think about finding a 'real' job.

There was then a dreadful interlude when an aunt persuaded me that it was my duty to teach in the village school, understaffed and overcrowded with children from London to such a pitch that an untrained volunteer would be welcome. I did it for two terms, proving that teaching was not my métier but that I could call upon a certain amount of courage at a pinch. It was during that time that I met the first of my 'hopeless' loves, felt myself blaze into life again—it was so good while it lasted that even when I think I can see its unreality, I do not regret it—and sank back into even colder ashes. By the time chance had put me on to a 'real' job in the B.B.C., I was far from being alive.

It is strange to remember that when I was at Oxford, the B.B.C. had glamour. When, before going down, we visited the Appointments Board which was supposed to help us find jobs, one after another of us said, 'Well, I rather thought the B.B.C. . . . ,' only to be laughed to scorn. (Does anyone ever get a job through a University Appointments Board, I wonder? I have never known anyone who did.) This made me see it as a stronghold of rare and brilliant people, so that to join it, although far down in the submerged seven-eighths which never sees a microphone, struck me as extraordinary. I did it because my Oxford friend Margaret had found a job in its recruitment office and tipped me off when a vacancy for which I might be suitable occurred.

For a time I was still prepared to grant glamour to the greater part of the Corporation, for I never saw it. My section, the part of an information service attached to the part of the B.B.C. which broadcast to 'the Empire,' had been evacuated to Evesham. 'The Empire' included, endearingly, I always thought, the U.S.A., and it was some time before the Corporation got round to noticing this and changed the name of the Service. We worked in an ugly manor house overlooking Housman's Bredon Hill, and because we were a new development, without which the News Room and so on had managed successfully for many years, few people, to begin with, bothered to consult us. With this job I went into a curious hermit existence so drained of feeling that it seemed even more unreal than it was.

I became shy, a condition unfamiliar to me. We were scattered about Evesham in billets, with a couple of clubs at which we could meet each other. I went twice to one of the clubs and spoke to no one. Still assuming that they were all unusual and exceptionally intelligent people, and observing that they knew each other well, I felt that they would consider me drab and dull, and did not dare to make any claim on their attention. I went back to my billet and after that I never did anything in my spare time but read: not even when I had realized that most of these alarming people were middle-aged journalists of no particular distinction.

The only things that I enjoyed at Evesham were the beginnings of the early shift and the ends of the late one. We covered the hours from six in the morning until midnight, and the first and last person to be on duty worked alone. At half-past five in the dark of a winter morning, the B.B.C. bus would put me down at the Manor's gates and I would make my way slowly up the drive, picking up firewood as I went. Having lit a fire in the grate of what had been one of the best bedrooms, I would fetch tea and sausages from the canteen and eat them sitting on the floor, watching my fire prosper. It was cold to begin with, and still, since only a skeleton staff was on at that hour, none of them in our part of the house. There was something secret and amusing about those picnic breakfasts, as though I were a tramp squatting in abandoned premises, and that slightly dotty pleasure is the only one I can remember from that time.

When we were transferred back to London and had become an accepted part of the B.B.C.'s machinery, it became an ordinary job and lasted for five years, until after the end of the war. It was never an exciting one but it kept us busy. We were supposed to be able to answer any question at any time, and usually we could: an information service is only a matter of knowing where to look. I liked most of the women with whom I worked, and if there was one I did not like she was usually disliked by all of us; it is not a bad thing in a group, I discovered, to have one unpopular member who will act as catalyst on the others. I came to be head of the section after a time, having first been 'passed over' in favour of a more efficient girl, which was supposed to be a drama. I was only slightly pleased when she turned out to be less efficient than had been expected and at last went away to have a baby, while the other women said, 'It should have been you in the first place.' I liked their liking me (it was lucky that they did, for it was, in fact, they who kept the section running), but my concern for the work was barely skin-deep. My concern for anything, at that time, was barely skin-deep.

My life became no more closely knit with the war. Paul was killed, but he had already gone away from me. A cousin was killed, but he was younger than I was and I had never been very close to him. Other people I knew were killed, but they did not belong to my daily life. These deaths were as though the poisonous atmosphere had condensed for a moment and a drop had fallen: horrible, but natural. The nearest violence came to my own person was when a room I was to sleep in that night was blown in, and when the curtains of another room suddenly, silently, bellied towards me, sweeping a china bowl off the window sill, and I had time to wonder whether I was having hallucinations before the sound of the explosion followed. I was not even affected by whatever feverish gaiety there may have been about (people speak of it in memoirs); it did not come my way. Years of emptiness. Years leprous with boredom, drained by the war of meaning. Other people's experience of them was far more painful, more dramatic, more tragic, more terrible than that; but that too, in its small, dim way, was hell.

During that time my soul shrank to the size of a pea. It had never been very large or succulent, or capable of sending out sprouts beyond the limits of self, but now it had almost shrivelled away. I became artful in avoiding pain and in living from one small sensation to another, because what else could one do when one had understood that, as far as one's personal life was concerned, one was a failure, doomed to be alone because one did not merit anything else, and when every day a part of one's job was to mark the wartime papers? I remember particularly a cutting about an elderly Pole who had killed himself, leaving a letter to say that he had tried everything to make people see what must be done for Poland but no one would listen. He was killing himself because it was the only gesture left him by which he might be able to draw people's attention to what was happening. He was a man who chose the other way, the opposite way to mine, and the poor old fanatic got about an inch and a half in a corner of the *Manchester Guardian.* If one were not to be a walking Francis Bacon picture, a gaping bloody mouth rent open in a perpetual scream, what could one do but go to the cinema and be grateful for an amusing film; go to bed and feel the smoothness of the sheets and the warmth of the blankets; go to the office and laugh because Helen's lover was at home on leave and she had asked Kathleen to say, if her mother telephoned, that she was staying with her. After the late shift the tiny sequins of the traffic lights, reduced by masks during the blackout, changed from red to amber to green down the whole length of empty, silent Oxford Street. They looked as though they were signalling a whispered conversation, and they were the kind of thing with which I filled my days.

Some people take refuge from emptiness in activity and excesses. They are the ones, I suppose, who cannot sleep for it. Mine was a dormouse escape, a hibernation. Instead of being unable to sleep I slept to excess, thinking lovingly of my bed during the day and getting into it with pleasure. Sleep for me has always been dreamless yet not negative, as though oblivion were a consciously welcomed good, so the only thing to dread about my nights was the slow, heavy emergence from them when an unthinking lack of enthusiasm for the days into which they pitched me made getting up an almost intolerable effort. Sleep at night, and a cautious huddling within limits during the day: walking to work along the same streets, eating the same meals, going back to the same room, then reading. In theory I longed to depart from this pattern and felt sorry for myself when I did not, but although I would have liked to have lived differently, the smallest alteration seemed to be beyond my energies. I had to be feeling unusually *well* before I could go so far as to take a bus to the National Gallery on a day off, instead of sleeping all the morning and reading all the afternoon.

Within these absurd limitations imposed on me by inertia, there were palliatives to be found: the company of the few friends then accessible—and that I do not say more about my friends is because their lives are their own affair, not because they are not precious to me—and the books I read, and the little life spun within the walls of the office, which was often amusing. The intimacy between people working together is an agreeable thing and very real, in spite of the disconcerting way in which it vanishes as soon as the same people meet each other in different circumstances. And always, at any time, I could look at things, whether at leaves unfolding on a plane tree, or at people's faces in a bus, or at a pigeon strutting after its mate on a roof, or at pictures. Perhaps the nearest I came to being fully alive for months on end was when I was looking at pictures. This joy I owe partly to the natural acuteness of my response to visual images and partly to one of my aunts, the only one of my mother's sisters to remain unmarried and the only one of them to escape from the family's way of thinking.

An intelligent and sensitive girl, she was extremely shortsighted and had to wear glasses. It was this, I believe, that caused her, as well as the rest of the family, to think her plain in spite of looks which by present-day standards would be considered striking. As a child she had stammered, and quite early in her life she must have written herself off as a shy and unattractive girl. She went to Oxford and became the family bluestocking, much loved by everyone but little understood. Her greatest friend became an almoner in a hospital, and my aunt followed her example. They shared a flat in London, decorated with hand-woven materials and reproductions of Impressionist paintings, and they worked with dedication and enjoyment.

When my grandfather knew that he was about to die, he told his daughter that she must give up her work and come back to Beckton to look after her mother. No one questioned this. My grandmother must have been about sixty at the time, an extraordinarily healthy, able woman whose house was constantly filled by visiting children and grandchildren. With a little planning she need hardly ever have been alone, and she had a character strong enough to withstand loneliness if it had to. But according to her ideas of what was fitting, it was taken for granted that an unmarried daughter owed a duty to her parents compared to which her duty to her work was frivolous and her duty to herself did not exist. My mother, the other sisters, and their brother shared this belief. Their own children were still young and they had not yet foreseen their own acceptance (in my mother a splendidly generous one) of their daughters' rights to lives of their own. 'It horrifies me now,' my mother has said to me. 'How *could* we have let her be sacrificed like that? But at the time it just seemed natural.'

What my aunt felt about it she never said. She was not only a reserved woman, but the most genuinely unselfish person I have ever met. Silent, a little apart, she threw herself into work. She gardened, she served on committees, she taught Sunday school in the village, she became a Justice of the Peace. The books on her shelves were not quite like the books of the rest of the family, the pictures in her bedroom were not like their pictures, and she was the only one who would slip away for holidays abroad, walking in the Dolomites, or staying in rough inns in Italy or Yugoslavia. She loved small children and they loved her. Gently, diffidently, she dropped crumbs of poetry or romanticism or liberal opinion along their paths for them to pick up if they cared to. One of these crumbs was an occasion when she took me up to London to a great exhibition of French painting given in Burlington House in the early 'thirties.

I have never forgotten that exhibition. To be in London was exciting enough, and to be doing something so grown-up as visiting an exhibition was even better: I was ready to enjoy the pictures, and enjoy them I did. I loved the Watteaus and the Fragonards, which seemed to me glimpses of an exquisitely graceful life in which I longed to join, but the canvases which impressed me as the most beautiful of the lot were *La Source* and *La Belle Zélie* by Ingres. That marmoreal perfection, that polished, heightened realism of texture, conveyed to me Ideal Beauty. Why did my aunt stand for so much longer in front of a *baigneuse* by Renoir? Why did she say, undidactically as usual, that she thought it more lovely than the Ingres? I looked at it attentively and could only see a smudgy painting of a plain girl who was too fat and too red. But my darling aunt, who knew about pictures—she *did* like it better than *La Source,* I could see that without being told. So although I did not then *see* the Renoir, nor any of the other Impressionists except Manet's boy playing the fife, I understood that this was a limitation in myself, not in them: the first, the vital lesson for anyone who wants to enjoy painting. Looking at that Renoir was like meeting someone at a party and getting nowhere with him because one or both of you happen to be distrait. You do not discover until you meet again that he is going to be one of your best friends—but useless though the first meeting may have seemed, without it the second one would not have taken place.

There was another occasion, too, earlier than this, when my aunt dropped a hint about art and I picked it up. I was drawing horses, as I constantly did, when she leant over my shoulder and said, 'Draw a naked man—a man or a woman.' Disconcerted by a suggestion that seemed to me indecent, I hesitated. She, seeing what I was thinking, became embarrassed in her turn and said, 'Go on, you needn't put in his—er—his little arrangements if you don't want to.' So I drew a shapeless forked radish and she looked disappointed. I did not understand her fond hope that a child's eye would produce something original and alive, but I knew that I had failed in some way: that there was something of significance I should have been able to do with the human body instead of being embarrassed by it. When, after that, I looked at paintings of the nude, I was looking for beauty.

So my aunt and my own temperament equipped me with eyes, and seeing things remained, through the dreariest stretches of my life, a reason for living.

Another device for filling emptiness—a common one, difficult to consider with detachment—is promiscuity. Lack of energy prevented me from ranging about in pursuit of men, but if they turned up, I slept with them. I had started this soon after unhappiness set in, and if I am to be honest I must admit that I was less shrivelled when I was doing it than I was when I was not: when, for instance, during a long period at Evesham and in London, I was too cowed by the double blow I had received from love to do even that.

It always seemed to me that the factor of physical frustration on the simplest level, although it must have played its part, was much less important than the reassurance which came from the sense of being desired and the mitigation of boredom which came from having something *to do*. That I must iron my pretty dress and wash my best underclothes because on Friday the bell would ring and I would be going out to dinner with a man, however dull, was at least to appear to be living. It was going through the familiar motions, it was getting back into harness, even if the drive would not lead anywhere—and I was determined that it should not. Only in an encounter which contained no threat of serious emotion, no real relationship, could I, at that time, feel safe.

Sometimes these sorties were not to be regretted. If there was enough companionship and physical compatibility, a small expansion beyond the confines of my own predicament into another person's life was possible, some tenderness could be felt—and tenderness between bodies, though restricted, is real. At other times they were simply absurd, and I would be both amused and puzzled by them. I would meet a man with whom I had nothing in common, who was perhaps fat and garrulous, who told boring anecdotes and could not even dance well. He would make the first movements of a pass at me and I, a little warmed because he was behaving as though I were attractive, would make the first responses. Hands would be held under restaurant tables, or as we danced my body would yield to his pressure until our thighs were touching. At that point I would say to myself, 'Now steady! You do not want to go on with this, you know quite well that it will be deadly.' But whatever reason might be saying, once the first moves had been made there was no breaking the pattern. It was as though a familiar music had begun to play, I had stepped into a familiar measure, and to go against its rhythm was beyond me. A certain kind of look, certain words, gestures, and contacts, and all my faculties would go into a state of suspension: bed was the only conclusion. 'What is *obliging* me to do this?' I would wonder, going up in a hotel lift or watching someone who should have been a stranger as he put his keys and change on a dressing-table. I would split in two on those occasions, one half going obediently and easily through the routine, the other watching with an ironic amusement. When the dance had reached its inevitable conclusion and the night in bed with whoever it might be was over, the two halves would rejoin and I would wake up thinking, 'But I am mad! Never again!'

This was where complications could set in. Common courtesy would have seemed to me, during the night, to demand that if I was making love with this man I should appear to enjoy it, so how, without insulting him, could I avoid a repetition? He would be under the impression that he had met a girl of easy virtue and amorous temperament, and would look forward to other meetings. I used to be forced to spin elaborate tales of my own fickleness, neuroticness, bitchiness—'You are well rid of me really, I promise.' Once, becoming hopelessly enmeshed in my own tangled web, I implied that it was only the man's ardour that had demolished my normally strong defences, whereupon he believed me and soon afterwards asked me to marry him: perhaps the most disconcerting thing that has ever happened to me.

These foolish and always short affairs were threadbare rags against a cold wind, but they were better than no rags at all. During the period when my spirits were too low for me to grasp at them, the shrivelling affected my body as well as my soul, my health deteriorated, my appetite dwindled, and sensations of faintness and nausea attacked me whenever I left my room or the office. I reached the stage of dreading the short walk between the two for fear that I should faint or vomit in the street. I went to a doctor, was told that I had become anaemic, and was sent home for a month's sick leave.

Beckton could always restore me. I used to imagine a 'scientific' reason for it: that the nature of its soil made its leaves and grasses give off a certain kind of exhalation which suited me above all others. But although as I sat in the train returning to London I felt better physically, I knew that at bottom I was the same: I would continue my dreary round unless I took some kind of action. 'It is not that life has deserted you,' I told myself. 'It is you who have deserted life.' I thought of the brisk injunctions in women's magazines—'Take up an interest,' 'Join a club.' At that sort of thing I could only laugh or shudder, it was too far outside my line of country. So I said to myself (it is not an inspiring thing to recall, but it is true)—I said to myself, 'Look, the next man you meet who appears at all attracted to you, whatever he is like, however unreal he seems to you, you will revert to your bad old ways and will accept whatever happens.'

I went straight from the station to the office, for the late shift. After a little gossip the girls I was relieving collected their things and left me alone in the racket of typewriters and ticker-tape machines from the News Room next door which had come to seem like silence.

I was about to go to the canteen for a coffee when the door opened and there stood a man whom I shall call Felix, a great womanizer and until recently the lover of a friend of mine who had left for a job abroad. 'Hullo, sweetie,' he said. 'Are you all alone?' A stocky little figure leaning against the door post, crinkling professional charmer's eyes. 'Yes,' I said. 'What can I do for you?' 'You can come out for a drink with me.' 'No, I can't, not until midnight, anyway.' 'All right, I'll come and collect you at midnight.'

Felix was anchored by marriage and was not a man whom I could admire enough to love. With him I could feel absolutely safe. At the same time he was a gay companion and we shared great pleasure in making love. Our relationship was pure *cinq-à-sept*, except that its venue was a restaurant where we would eat as good a dinner as could be found in wartime London, and drink a lot, before going to spend a night in an hotel or, if Felix's family was in the country, at his house. Neither of us ever set foot in each other's daily life. We would bring to our meetings incidents from it, if they were amusing or bizarre, but neither ever expected the other to take more than a passing interest in anything more grave; I would never, for example, have told Felix about money troubles except as a joke, and he would hardly have referred to any difficulties he might be having with his children. Our roles were clearly defined: to make each other laugh, and to give each other physical pleasure. At both of these he was very good. He was an excellent raconteur with a quick eye for character and an immense relish for the absurd, whose sympathies, though not profound, were wide. He had also the disarming honesty with which a rake will often feel that he can justify himself. He loved having money and making a vulgar show with it, because to make a show was more fun than being discreet. He loved success, even though he had got it by jettisoning his integrity as a writer. The relish with which he lived eclipsed any thought of how he might have lived.

I had become so emotionally impotent because of the tension between a conscious longing to love and a subconscious fear of it that my feelings for anyone, for a long time, had gone no further than a detached well-wishing. Towards Felix I could feel a positive affection, and it was not—most certainly it was not—to be despised. For two years I remained his mistress (or, more probably, one of his mistresses), and only put an end to it when restored vitality and confidence pushed me out again on to the perilous waters of deeper feeling. And although I was to capsize yet again, my years with Felix had made me more buoyant. With him I had been happy, though in an inglorious way, and I was by that much less likely to drown.

I wish I had never met Felix again after we had separated, but I did. Eight years later the telephone rang and I heard that familiar, husky voice, that contented chuckle, and cried, 'Felix! Come round at once!' As I opened the door to him I thought 'Heavens, he must have been having a hard day,' because he had something about him a little dishevelled and awry that I had never seen. Then I noticed a smell of alcohol—stale alcohol—that was almost sickening. 'He is drunk,' I thought with surprise, for in spite of all the whisky we had put away together I had never seen him drunk. We went out to dinner, and as the evening passed I realized slowly that this was no unfortunate chance. The bartender had greeted him with bored patience instead of with the old comradely twinkle, the head waiter had given us an obscure table, and no wonder, because Felix started making bawdy jokes, very loud. At one point, when he had eaten a little, he appeared to pull himself together and began to talk as he used to talk and to ask me questions about myself, but I soon realized that he was unable to listen to the answers. When he screwed up his eyes at me it was horrible—the scrag-end of charm, ossified with exploitation. Deliberately frivolous as he was, a hedonist, an opportunist, vulgar in some ways though with a flourish that seemed to me to redeem it, my dear Felix should have been able to bob his way merrily into old age in defiance of Nemesis, but he could not. When he died soon afterwards, people said it was from drink, and I could only suppose it to be so: a man who had actually said in my hearing, 'Don't be silly, you know that I can take it or leave it alone'; a man who would have detested himself in the role of object lesson for any end other than merriment or pleasure. I suppose he is an odd person towards whom to feel gratitude and tenderness, but those are the emotions his memory will always bring to life in me. Felix enjoyed women so much that he could not help making them feel valuable, indeed he would have considered it amateurish not to do so. It was he who began the slow process of my restoration.

13

THE SQUARE, SCRUBBED woman with cropped hair sat behind a desk on which was a vase of catkins. Her consulting room was decorated in cream and green, a combination I detest.

'Well, now,' she said in a voice intended to nip hysteria in the bud, 'it's not the end of the world.'

I had never thought it was. She saw, I supposed, a great many unmarried women who had become pregnant, so that she could hardly have avoided treating them according to formula, but I began at once to resent that she was applying her formula to me.

'In fact,' she went on, 'one might almost say that in wartime, when there is such a shortage of beds in the maternity wards and so on, it is simpler to have a baby when you are not married than when you are.'

'Oh?' I said.

'Yes, there is a lot of help available. I would strongly advise you to go on with it. It's your natural function and if you frustrate it you will find that a trauma results, a profound trauma. And it's quite simple when you have made up your mind to it—there are plenty of war widows about. You can change your job and wear a wedding ring and no one will suspect a thing.'

'But what about afterwards, when the baby is born?'

'That's the simplest part,' she said. 'I can put you in touch with organizations to look after that. There are three alternatives. One: you have the baby and its adoption is arranged beforehand. You won't even see it. The committee is extremely careful in its vetting of couples who want to adopt children—we make sure that they really want them, as well as that they are able to support them, and I can assure you that it is pure sentimentality to worry about the child in that case. It will probably be a good deal better off with its adopted parents than it would be with you.' She laughed as she spoke: little shocks of briskness were the thing.

'I don't see much point,' I said, 'in going through nine months of pregnancy and a birth, and not even *seeing* my child after all that.' I had a vivid mental picture of waking in a hospital bed to an emptiness through which I could never crawl.

'No. Well then, there's the second alternative: foster parents. We find a foster mother for it and you are free to see it whenever you like, and then, when you are in a better position to look after it, when you are making more money or have got married, you can take it back. You would be surprised at the number of men who can be made to accept such a situation.'

What, I thought, if I never make any more money, or never get married, or can't make a husband accept the situation? And what of a child brought up by a woman who must seem to be its real mother, only to be snatched away by someone who has been no more than a visitor? It was less intolerable than the first prospect but not something I would risk. I nodded and looked expectant.

'The third solution,' she said, 'is to my mind much the best. You take your parents into your confidence straight away and get them to help you keep the child. What have you got against that?'

'My parents,' I said. 'They would be horrified.'

'Do them good, silly old things,' said the woman.

I looked at her in astonishment. She was speaking of people of whom she knew nothing—not their ages, nor their income, nor their way of life, nor their feelings towards their daughter—so how could she possibly presume to know whether it would do them good or not? Her high-handed dismissal of my parents as 'silly old things' was a piece of gross impertinence. I sat there thinking 'What a frightful woman!' while she went on to explain that most families, once an illegitimate child becomes a *fait accompli,* adapt themselves to the situation after a time, however shocking they find it at first. 'You would probably find,' she said, 'that it would become your mother's favourite grandchild. I have seen that happen.'

My reason told me that she was right: that if I were to go on with this, it would have to be on those terms. I was earning only five pounds a week and could not save anything like enough money to make me independent. Someone would have to help me, and the child's father was not able to. It was probably true that my parents, after their first horror and distress, would come round to taking the responsibility—but if they did, it would only be at a great cost both emotionally and financially. Their lives as well as mine would be disrupted and complicated, and it seemed to me outrageous that I, because of my own folly, should force them into such a situation. This pregnancy was my business and no one else's.

'No,' I said.

'Well,' said the woman, 'you will regret it terribly if you have an abortion. You're in perfect shape physically—I would say that yours is an ideal pregnancy, so far. You will suffer in every way if you terminate it.' She looked down at her hands, then reached out to straighten a folder on her desk. When she looked up, her eyes were sharp with calculation. 'It is, of course,' she went on slowly, 'entirely your own business. It is entirely up to you if you want'—she paused a moment to throw the verb into relief—'if you want *to murder* your first child'—and she watched me.

'Yes, it is,' I said, getting up. Her look, the choice of verb, had clarified my mind in a flash. I knew, now, that I must get on with the job of finding an abortionist.

Walking down the street, I began to laugh. 'The old black-mailer!' I thought. 'Murder, indeed!' Applied to an embryo two and a half months developed, the word, I was abruptly convinced, was nonsense. What was happening in my womb was still simply a physiological process concerning only me, a new departure of my body's. Later there would be a creature there to consider, but at this stage—no.

I had become pregnant by subconscious intention and had recognized the fact clearly as soon as it had happened. I had felt brilliantly well from the first day, and proud. I was already having fond dreams of babies in their prams, I knew that I wanted one, I knew that my body had plotted in order to achieve what it most needed—and not only my body but the subconscious layers of my mind. Until I had visited that woman I had seriously been considering bearing the child, but now I knew, without regret, that I would not. The birth of a child was not a matter of therapy for the mother. Would I have a trauma as a result of frustrating it? Too bad for me if I did. I was not going to become a mother unless I could do it properly.

As it turned out, the suffering of which the woman had warned me never materialized. Physically my health was distinctly improved by three months of pregnancy followed by a curettage, and any trauma that may have resulted has yet to manifest itself. I have often regretted my childlessness and I have caught myself up to my tricks again in attempts to remedy it, but neither of the two attitudes I thought likely have developed: I have never yearned over other people's children, nor have I recoiled from them. I like them, I enjoy their company, I find them interesting, and that seems to be that. I can only suppose that by nature I am a maternal woman but not passionately so.

How far did laziness and self-indulgence come into my decision? That they did so to some extent I am sure. One of the many strands of feeling running through me as I sat in that consulting room was certainly dismay at the prospect of having to find a new job and new lodgings, of having to uproot myself (although from a life which I knew to be empty and dull) and turn to solving practical difficulties outside my experience. My inertia was heavy on me, making me reluctant to face the inevitable complications of my situation. I was partly a coward, and a coward in the face of effort, rather than of anything else.

But although it is probable that my justification of my attitude was—and is—to some extent an attempt to rationalize this lack of spirit, the other elements in my argument did exist. It still seems to me that it is absurd for abortion to be illegal. I do not believe that something not conscious can be 'murdered'—the distinction between preventing life and putting an end to it is, to me, a clear one. Other women who bear the full consequences of their actions I admire and even, if they make a success of it, envy. Whether they have argued that life must be respected, or whether (which is, I imagine, more often the case) they have obeyed the dictates of their own hungers, they show a courage which I lacked. But in bestowing on a child the chancy fate of illegitimacy, they have shouldered a heavy responsibility. Only if I felt myself able to offer it security would I do it myself, and such security I could not offer at that time.

So I say, so I believe: but supposing the woman behind the desk had been one who, while putting forward the same arguments, had not alienated me by her manner, had spoken to *me* instead of to a pregnant girl of her own invention? . . . The points, perhaps, would have been switched, my life would have veered on to another course. Even though reason was mixed with my weakness to a point where they are hard to disentangle, it does not quite raise it above regret. I am glad that I did not risk giving a child a difficult life, but I am sorry that I was not the kind of girl who would have braved that risk.

14

THE WAR WAS in its third year or perhaps the beginning
of its fourth. I was still working in the B.B.C., slightly better at living by then, since Felix was a part of my life and
I had left bed-sitting rooms behind me for a flat which I shared
with another girl—a commonplace event which must be remembered by millions of working women as a turning-point in their
lives. Who could feel their circumstances anything but temporary,
their condition anything but one of time-biding, while the daily
mechanics of living consist of eating only what can be boiled on a
gas-ring (frying is usually forbidden because of the smell and the
spitting of fat on to the carpet), keeping half one's clothes in a suit-
case under the divan or on top of the wardrobe, moving books and
writing things from a table to a divan or chair before setting out a
meal, and turning a divan from couch into bed every night before
going to sleep in the froust of one's cigarette smoke? I had taken
a modest pride in my ingenuity with small bed-sitting rooms, the
way in which I could make myself comfortable and control the

ebullience of my too numerous possessions; so much so that when I first experienced the delicious freedom of a flat, I was astonished by the violence with which I cast off single-room living. I had not known that it had been horrible, but it was with horror that I decided 'Never again!'

In a flat we could give parties. To one of them a friend brought a small Hungarian said to be in publishing. He did not seem to be much amused by our company, although he did not whisper audibly, as I have heard him do since then, 'Can we go now?' He sat on the floor looking boyish and disdainful, then sang 'The Foggy Foggy Dew' in a manner implying that he, personally, had discovered this song. When he telephoned a few days later to invite me to a play, I was surprised. I was also pleased because I believed that anyone connected with publishing must be interesting.

It did not take us long to decide that our relationship would not be an amorous one. Instead we slipped into a friendship of a curiously intimate nature, nearer to the fraternal than anything I had experienced within my family. My real brother, with whom I had been close friends when we were small, had been taken out of my life first by his schooling, then by what his schooling had done to him. He had hated it and had spent much of his boyhood taking refuge in stupidity and near-oafishness, happy only when disguised as a gamekeeper or, better still, poacher, wearing an ancient, many-pocketed waistcoat, talking dialect, and sloping about the woods at Beckton either alone or with friends from the village. By the time he began to emerge from this camouflage I was at Oxford, and after that the war removed him. On the rare occasions when we met there was always a comfortable freedom between us, an ability to say or to listen to anything and a clear view of each other's shortcomings which did not prevent affection, but we did not have much in common beyond our temperaments and our memories. With the Hungarian, André Deutsch, I shared a way of life, political views, and interest in the arts, as well as an undemanding kind of intimacy very similar to that I already knew with my brother.

We began to see each other often and became, in a lopsided way, each other's confidants: lopsided because while I had a tendency to underestimate my own value, André had no doubt about his. He was always ready to put himself out for friendship's sake in any practical way—lend money, or bring round food if I were in bed with influenza—but he did not find it easy to believe that I (or anyone else) would be as interested in a discussion of my own life as I would be in his.

He had come to England before the war broke out, ostensibly to complete his education but with a private determination to settle here. With liberal views and a Jewish father, he had decided while still a boy that Hungary under Horthy was not the country he would have chosen, whereas English literature, combined with everything he had heard about Great Britain, suggested to him that England was. So early and complete a transference of loyalties, made without any great pressure from events, seems to me unusual and strange. André had reacted to things which were in the air rather than to anything which had happened to him or his family. When I have questioned him about it he has answered no more than 'I just knew, always, that that was what I wanted to do.' Caught by the war, with no money but an occasional cheque from an uncle in Switzerland, he picked up jobs here and there and was working as floor manager in a big hotel when detectives came to remove him to the Isle of Man. To be an enemy alien was not, however, an unmixed evil. Internment did not last long, and once he was released he was free to take what civilian work he liked, provided he reported at the proper times to the Aliens' Office. He found his way by chance into the sales side of an old—indeed tottering—publishing house, and by the time I met him he had burrowed well into its structure, was saving a little money, and was already talking of starting a firm of his own.

André was my age—twenty-six. By that time he did not have a penny beyond what he earned, nor did he have a single relative, old friend, or useful connection in this country. I used to listen to his plans indulgently, contributing to them as one contributes to talk about what one will do when one wins the Irish Sweep. 'If you join me,' he said to me one day as we walked arm-in-arm through Soho, 'what would be the minimum money you would have to earn, to be comfortable?'

'I don't know,' I said. 'What am I earning now?' And he worked out for me, as he has so often done since, what my weekly salary came to by the year. It was three hundred and eighty-eight pounds, I believe—the B.B.C. paid civil-service rates and Temporary Women Clerks, the category under which I worked, did not come high in those rates.

'What about five hundred pounds?' he asked, and I agreed to it, feeling that such a large sum could safely be considered since it existed only in his imagination. I had not yet understood that André is the kind of person in whom ideas and action are inseparable. It is true that when the time came, five hundred pounds proved at first to have been optimistic—but the time did come.

I have sometimes wondered whether, if chance had shouldered André into property, or manufacturing cars, or catering, his obsessive nature would have seized on that as it did on publishing. Perhaps it would have done, but it is hard to believe. Picture dealing, maybe, or concert promoting. . . . The nature of his talent is practical, the demon which possesses him is a business demon rather than a literary one, yet it is impossible to imagine it functioning for an end unconcerned with artistic expression. The ultimate good for a business demon *ought* to be power through money, but André's demon drives for something else. He is immensely concerned with money, but as an idea rather than as something to possess: while he can have a car and good clothes he is indifferent to his own income. He will cry out in pain at the least mistake in the costing of a book or the most trivial slip in his opponent's favour during a deal, but the pain is aesthetic rather than pecuniary: he is offended in the way that a stylist is offended by a badly constructed sentence or an interior decorator by an ugly juxtaposition of objects. The only power without which he cannot live is that of being his own master—over other people he exercises it both reluctantly and clumsily. His business demon is one which, by some quirk, has become bound to the production of books so firmly that its energy would bleed away if it were cut off from them. Whatever he may say when he feels resentful at the demands of his own obsession, André is a man with a vocation.

No two people could be more different than he and I. He has the most exact and capacious memory I have ever encountered, while I can remember hardly anything but people and feelings; he is a fiend for detail, while I am sloppy; he has this instinctive understanding of money and what can be done with it—the structure of a company, the financing of a new enterprise, are things which he can grasp at once without any previous experience—while to me the simplest

contract is sterile: words on paper which I can understand if I concentrate but which have no implications beyond the mere statement,
none of which I can criticize in relation to a set of ideas. André has
the sometimes blinkered driving force of the obsessive, to whom his
own ends are both *necessary* and *right*. I have the detachment of the
disassociated, always prepared to believe that the other side of the
question may have something in it. Above all, André is active, he
compels things to happen, while I am passive, I accept. It is easier for
me to see what I have gained from our long partnership than it is to
understand why he values it.

As soon as the war was over, André formed his company: Allan
Wingate, it was called, we picked the name out of a hat in the
belief that 'Deutsch' would still meet with prejudice. I had to round
off my work at the B.B.C. and then took a three-months holiday
at Beckton, so I did not join him until 1946 and cannot exactly
remember how the absurdly small capital was raised. It was little
more than three thousand pounds. Part of it, I know, came from
a man who made handbags, who liked books and who had sized
up André as a young man who would go far. Printers, binders, and
papermakers reached the same conclusion, allowing him generous
credit and taking extraordinary trouble to be helpful. Partly they
were charmed, for André is capable of exerting great charm, and
partly they were convinced, because absolute conviction breeds conviction. It is fortunate that André is by inclination honest, for if he
were a liar he would be one of those mesmeric pathological liars
whose fabrications dupe everyone for years, simply because such liars
believe in them themselves.

Our first office was two rooms, a passage, a w.c. and a box-room with a skylight next to the w.c. in which sat a sequence of morose little men who did our accounts. That they were morose was not surprising. The chief thing that I remember about those first few years was the agony of bills coming in: the agony of paying them when we had to, and the agony of not paying them when we could get away with it. There is at all times a sum without which, the pontiffs say, you cannot launch a publishing house. It stood in those days at fifteen thousand pounds—five times what André had been able to raise—and stands today at fifty thousand. At any period I am sure that this sum can safely be halved by anyone prepared to work hard, while by fanatics it can probably be quartered. But in cutting it by five we had gone too near the knuckle. What was to happen later could still have been avoided, but the need to avoid it would not have arisen if we had begun with more capital.

Meanwhile, in spite of money worries, we enjoyed ourselves. We made a few mistakes, published one or two of those handsome editions on handmade paper, illustrated with woodcuts by expensive artists and bound in buckram, which few people can resist producing when they first get their hands on the means of book-making and which never earn their keep. But for the most part we managed, thanks to André's vigilance over every halfpenny, to produce our books at an economic price, and we succeeded, after great difficulties, in organizing their distribution on the right lines. That our overheads should have been unnecessarily high by as little as a pound would have shocked us all: 'Have you switched off your fire?' 'Why are you using a new envelope for this, don't you know what stickers are *for?*' We kept our stock in the passage leading to the w.c. where a narrow bench had been installed, and there, just before a publication date, the whole firm would stand, working away with sticky paper and string, under the benevolent eye of our real packer, Mr Brown.

Mr Brown would always have to accompany whoever it was who was making the London deliveries in André's small car, because only a Union member could hand a parcel of books to another Union member. I used to enjoy my turn on deliveries, listening to a gentle burble of London lore, for Mr Brown, a compulsive talker, prided himself that he knew every inch of the city, and so he did. His interpretations of what he knew were sometimes eccentric, museums becoming cathedrals, and monuments commemorating events that had happened or people who had existed long after they were erected. Strange things went on in Mr Brown's London, too: men in Islington bit off the heads of rats for a shilling, and there was a building near Westminster Cathedral full of holy images covered with blood—'You know, all Christ and bloody Mary and that.' When I asked him how he knew, he told me that he had once spent a whole night there, packing singlehanded to oblige, and that all these images with the blood on them had got him down so much that he didn't half let out a yell when the bishop came in at three o'clock in the morning to offer him a glass of wine. 'Wine, that's what he called it, but if you ask me it wasn't nothing of the kind.' When I laughed and said, 'Do you mean that he was trying to poison you?' he answered, 'Well, I don't know that I'd go so far as to say *that*,' but in a doubtful voice. And then, he said, when morning came, a great many women arrived, all dressed in black from top to toe, and all of them crying as though heartbroken. Mr Brown often left his stories hanging at a point like that, but I was so disturbed by all these sad, black-clad women that I persuaded him to explain them. 'Well, they was all rank Catholics, you see,' he said, 'and some old cardinal had kicked the bucket. I tried to jolly them along, I did. You wouldn't see me taking on like that, I said, not for him anyway, he's just another man to me. Cor, they didn't half think me a *vile* man.'

Mr Brown called me by my first name, but I would have felt it impertinent to have addressed him by his—André was the only person who ever did. He was a fatherly man, and kind, although his kindness could be disconcerting. 'No,' he said, 'I don't hold with giving up my seat in a bus to a young girl, she's as fit to stand as I am, only when she's having her monthly I will.' 'But Mr Brown, how can you tell?' 'Tell? I can always tell. Tell at a glance with the lot of you, I can.' The intimacy of a small business is certainly no myth.

The firm prospered, in that the books coming its way became better and that we were selling the right number of them, but in publishing money goes out fast and comes in slowly, and we had no margin. Every now and then the bills would heap up beyond the danger point and something would have to be done. There would be a short period of blank despair when we faced the fact that none of us knew anyone with money, and then André would pick up a scent. Someone, it would turn out, did know someone who had heard of someone who had always wanted an interest in a publishing firm (once it was a manufacturer of lavatory seats). I have learnt by now that there is *always* someone about who wants such an interest, but in those days it used to seem a miracle. Meetings would be arranged, friendships would flare up, and a new director, more or less active as the case might be, would appear on the Board.

The trouble with directors recruited by André in this way—and at our peak we had six of them—was that they thought of themselves, not unreasonably, as directors, while we thought of them as stooges. I had no official finger in the pie at that time, being only an employee, not a partner, but because I knew André so well and had been working with him almost from the beginning, I was his close ally, no more willing than he was to see anyone else in control of a firm so essentially his own. Only the last man to join the Board had any practical experience of publishing, and none of them had anything like André's flair, eye for detail, or capacity for hard work.

André had been drawn to England by a romantic conception of it, and this he still retained. Confront him with an Hungarian goose and he would see it for what it was, but his English geese always began as swans. This led him into the folly of agreeing to 'a gentleman's agreement' instead of to a service agreement when we reached the ticklish point at which one of the infiltrating directors acquired fifty-one percent of the shares in the company: the words 'a *gentleman's* agreement' sounded to André so much more British. That such an agreement should work when the other party, although having financial control, was expected to play the role of office boy (as he plaintively remarked) was a vain hope.

Tact was needed: tact, restraint, easygoing dispositions on both sides, and equal or complementary abilities all round. These conditions were lacking. The firm, while becoming outwardly more prosperous every day, deteriorated into a state of guerrilla warfare. I blush for us now, when I remember the spirit with which we entered into it, but I still cannot see how either André or I could have continued to work with any pleasure or profit except on his terms.

After five years of hard work we had moved our office to a charming house in Knightsbridge; we had published some good and successful books; we were making a profit; we were at home in our trade: and there we sat in our office (all right, we would have acknowledged crossly, the money was not ours but without us there would have been no office at all) in what, by the last painful weeks of a painful year, amounted to a state of siege.

During that year tempers had worn quite away. One of our directors would draft a contract and André, always quick to scent danger, would pick it off his desk. 'Are you mad?' he would cry— and that the oversight he had spotted was a grave one did not make his intervention more acceptable. Another of them would write a blurb and I would take it upstairs and rewrite it without consulting him. That his version was embarrassing, and that he would not have agreed to alter it if I had asked him, did not prevent my action from being high-handed. And in the usual way, inexperience and ineptitude became clumsier for being jumped on, so that the jumping daily seemed more necessary. Soon we had reached the point of dissecting each other's characters with morbid relish behind each other's backs, then of rival factions taking each other out for a drink in attempts at conciliation, only to come back to the office with new foibles to dissect. One of our directors wept easily after his third drink. He did not seem to notice it, but tears would spill out of his round blue eyes and smear his broad face as he catalogued the insults he had received. I would feel sorry for him and for a moment would really believe that I was discussing ways of improving our relationship, but all the time I was watching this extraordinary spectacle with secret glee, ready to caricature it as soon as André and I were alone together. I doubt whether unhappy marriages bring out the worst in people any more surely than unhappy business partnerships.

The frightening thing about a situation such as this one is that when recriminations begin about recent events, two people, each absolutely convinced that he is speaking the truth, will advance two opposite versions of a conversation or a happening. When that point has been reached no intermediary—and several were called in—can bridge the gap. Once meetings start being held in lawyers' offices, you might as well give up.

We did not give up until everyone was shut in his separate room, communicating only through secretaries. At that point André had to allow himself to admit that he had no choice: the other man had financial control, André did not have a service agreement, 'gentleman' was a word that could hardly have been applied to any of us at that moment—we were beaten.

I cannot remember where it was that André and I sat down to digest the fact, but I have an impression that there was a table between us, with white cups on it. 'Well,' he said, 'what do we do now?' We looked at each other and it was hardly necessary to speak the words. There was nothing we could possibly do but start another publishing firm.

That André should have had no doubts about this was only natural, but that I should have felt as he did suggests that I had become, if not a career woman, at least a woman who had found a career. And so, I suppose, I had. I would have preferred, and I would still prefer, not to have to work for my living in an office, but if I must, then a publisher's office is the one to be in. The formation and progress of the new firm, in which our friend Nicolas Bentley and I became and remained the only working directors beside André, is a story to be kept in reserve in case André should one day want to write it, but if I am ever to say what I like about the game, I should be able to say it now.

Book X is not so good as Book Y. Books A, B, and C have good reasons for their existence but do not happen to interest me. Books D and E—God knows what we were thinking of when we took those on, they will both flop and they deserve to flop. Book F is embarrassing—I do not like it, I do not think it good, but it will make a lot of money and it is not actually pernicious. But books G, H, I, J, and K: now there are books with which I am pleased to have been concerned, there are voices which deserve to be heard; and somewhere among them are my darlings, the books—not many of them, for in no generation are there many such writers—the books which, I believe, *had* to exist. This is why I like the work, and this is why other people in publishing like it, although some of them choose to affect a 'hard-headed-businessman' attitude and say at cocktail parties things like 'I never read books' or 'I can't stand writers.' If a publisher does not have a good head for business either on his own shoulders or on his partner's, he is a poor publisher, but if a good head for business were all he had, he would be making detergents or shoes or furnishing fabrics, not books.

Apart from that it is a job which suits me because it has a constant element of extemporization in it, if not lunacy. Its nature forbids the hardening of its arteries into routine. This often makes me bilious with rage, or sullen, or reckless: I long fiercely to know what it would be like to do work in which I could start something and be sure that

I could carry it through to the end uninterrupted. But against that, I am not often bored.

I used to have a dream of a pretty office. When I became a director, I imagined, I would acknowledge the fact that the greater part of my waking life is spent at work and I would have a room which gave me pleasure, with a wide enough desk, a comfortable chair, decorative objects on the shelves, colours I enjoyed on the walls, pictures and plants. For several weeks I relished the thought of this room, but the day I moved into it was the last day it looked pretty. A meticulously neat person—our third partner, Nicolas Bentley, for instance—can keep paper at bay, but not someone as untidy and lacking in method as myself, and while most work involves paper, mine produces things made of it as well. How does one control paper? Letters and copies of letters not yet filed because I must be reminded to do something about them; a layout pad, and loose sheets from it with rough sketches on them; periodicals and cuttings from periodicals; memoranda on the backs of used envelopes; lists of publication dates, of contracts signed, of changes in the prices of books, of advertising space bought, of people to invite to a party, of other people to whom complimentary copies are to be sent; samples of paper for book jackets or text; typescripts and synopses; reports on typescripts and synopses; proofs, both in galley and in page; roughs submitted by an artist for a jacket, or the finished art work roosting with me so that I remember to telephone the artist about a correction: a perpetual autumn sheds its paper leaves, heaping them on to my desk, drifting them into piles on my floor so that I cannot push my chair back without tumbling them. My reference books can never be dusted because of the paper lying on top of them and when I want my ruler, my scissors, or my india-rubber, my hands grope into the drifts on my desk and sheets of paper, unsettled, flutter to join the paper on the floor. Only outsize matchboxes and bumper tins of rubber solution are any good to me. The smaller sizes would submerge with the bottles of coloured ink, the roll of Scotch tape, and the pretty lustre shell which holds my paper clips. Only my type-gauge usually remains above paper, because if I cannot see it out of the corner of my eye I grow hysterical.

A type-gauge is a thin metal ruler marked with the units of measurements for type: twelve points to a pica; an eleven-point em is this long—; the type area of this page is twenty-four picas wide. The type in which this page is set is an eleven-point type, and there are four additional points of space between the lines. The type-gauge is one of the tools of the typographer and has no business on an editorial desk. But our firm, although it is growing too big to be called a small firm, still feels like one; not so long ago any of us might have had to turn our hand to anything, and we have got into the habit of it. Because I can draw after a fashion and enjoy problems of design, I was the one to whom it fell to lay out advertisements, through which I came to know enough to lay out a book if I had to, and to design odd jobs such as leaflets and showcards, and to criticize other people's designs. Nowadays, if the production department is overloaded, it will be to me that any overspill of designing comes. It is in this part of the work that one comes nearest to the actual making of a book as a physical object, that one learns something of the printer's, binder's, and blockmaker's problems. It is here that the element of craftsmanship comes in. Because this, like all making, is fascinating, my type-gauge has become a symbol of *being a bookmaker* as distinct from being a seller of books and an assessor of the merits of a writer's work, and of the three activities the making is the most comforting, the most sane in its procedures and dependable in its consequences.

So no sooner have I settled down to edit a typescript, or to read some unhappy writer's work which has been waiting for several weeks, than the internal telephone rings and the sales manager says, 'I promised Hatchards a showcard for such and such a book by the day after tomorrow. Is there any chance of it?' Pushing the typescript or book aside, I disinter the layout pad and begin to scrawl an idea to take to the sign-writer across the street (I shall have to take it across myself because I shall have to explain that the lettering is to be in such and such a style and that the girl is not supposed to have a squint although I have given her one). An idea is beginning to hatch when the telephone rings again: have I remembered that copy for our six-inch advertisement in the *Observer* has got to be sent in today, or have I made my notes yet on that draft letter to the lawyer about the possible libel action, or when will the blurb for the jacket of Book X be ready, or 'Mr Hackenpuffer is here with some drawings to show you, he says he has an appointment,' or 'There's a lady on the line who wants to submit a manuscript, only she says it's written in Polish so she must talk to an editor about it,' or 'Will you please speak to Mr Z, Mr Deutsch says he's out' (oh God, trouble!). On many days there comes a moment when a loud scream would be the only appropriate expression of feeling, and this is happening not only in my room but in André's room and in Nicolas Bentley's room (in spite of his neatness) and to some extent in all the other rooms. Even the specialists, snugly enclosed within their specialities—the sales manager, the production manager, the accountant, the chief invoicing clerk, the head packer—even they are dealing not with one process but with as many processes as there are books being produced and sold, for each book is a separate operation, with its own problems and timetable.

Many of the problems which beset a publishing firm do not come to me, but all of them are in the air. It is not a peaceful job.

In addition to the enjoyable liveliness which belongs to work unamenable to routine, there is another side of the job which I enjoy: meeting writers. An artist is not bound to be likeable and I have no doubt that many publishers could give examples of writers whose work they admired while they detested the authors as individuals. I have been lucky. Among the writers I have known, the better the artist, the more I have liked the man or woman. 'We are a neurotic lot, every last one of us,' one of them said to me, and certainly the good ones I have known have included the violently moody, the super-sensitive, the spiteful-about-other-people's-work, the hard drinker, the bad husband, the unable-to-communicate-in-speech, the cheerfully perverse, the conventionally amoral. Underneath whatever it may be, however, they have all had a private sanity which does not seem to me to be neurotic: they are the people to whom truth is important, and who can see things. The greatest pleasure I have found in publishing is in knowing such people.

The relationship is an easy one, because the publisher usually meets his writers only after having read something they have written, and if he has thought it good it does not much matter to him what the man will be like who is about to come through his door.

He is feeling well-disposed for having liked the work; the writer is feeling well-disposed for his work having been liked; neither is under obligation to attempt a close personal relationship beyond that. It is a warm and at the same time undemanding beginning, in which, if genuine liking is going to flower, it can do so freely. My own feeling, if I have been truly excited by a book, is nearer to a curiously detached kind of love than to liking: I have looked at the head of the man or woman sitting opposite me and thought, 'It all came out of that head,' and I could have taken it between my hands and kissed it. There cannot be many other kinds of middlemen whose wares inspire feelings so satisfying as that.

It did not surprise me to discover in myself, when I first went into publishing, this profound respect for good writing. I had not thought much about it before because I had not had occasion to use it, but it was always there. How could it not have been? It was not only a matter of being reared in a reading family, it was a matter of having lived, quite literally, a great part of my life entirely in terms of the printed word, or of images on canvas or on the screen.

It is a startling realization. To have lived from 1917 to 1961 and to have known violence only through the printed word or through images; to have known social injustice and revolution only through the printed word or through images; to have seen Jews stumbling down concrete steps into the gas chamber only through the printed word or through images; to have experienced fear, hunger, loss of liberty, or courage, relief from want and the impulse to fight for freedom only through the written word or through images: this is astounding. I remember that when shadows on a screen formed the sticklike limbs of Belsen protruding at awkward angles from piles of bodies, the feet grotesquely big at the end of legs shrunk to bone, I was engulfed in a terrible silence of unreality—my own unreality, not that of the shadows. In the same way books have been my windows on to vast tracts of experience, both destructive and creative, in which I have not lived. To the poet, to the painter, to the writer of serious prose as distinct from the entertainer (much though I owe to the latter), I am so much in debt that if artists did not exist, I cannot imagine that I would. I shall be grateful all my life to André Deutsch for having come to my party and thus steered me into a job in which I have been able to get to know a few of what seem to me by far the most real human beings in the world.

15

S O, WITH THE end of the war, work which I thought worth doing came my way. Had I been asked whether it made me happy, I would have answered 'Happy? No. But who is likely to have more than a few months of positive happiness during a lifetime?' That I was lucky I knew. My basic sense of failure was always present like a river bed, but the water running over the bed had become deeper than I had supposed it would ever be. My work brought enough incident and movement into my life for me to be content to exist with very little beyond that.

Of social life I had, and still have, almost none. I have never had a talent for acquaintance, only an enjoyment of intimacy. People who have more than three or four friends whom they wish to see often, who come and go to dinner parties and so on with a wide circle of acquaintances whose company they enjoy although they do not know them very well, fill me with envious admiration. When I was young I enjoyed parties so much that any was better than none—the murmur of voices and clink of glasses as I came up a staircase, the smell of the women's scent, the spurts of laughter, the sparkle of lights would delight me in themselves. Once during my twenties it occurred to me that a time would come when not only would I no longer dance but I would not *mind* not dancing, and I wept. But now, although I usually enjoy parties when I go to them (with the exception of large cocktail parties, which are the antithesis of social pleasure), I do not miss them, and I only missed them sharply in fits and starts during the years immediately after the war. Partly my seclusion came from lack of money and space, for I myself could not afford to entertain people other than casually, and partly it was the natural result of being a single woman moving into her thirties. Such new acquaintances as I made were usually married couples, most of whose friends were other married couples, and the occasions on which a spare woman can be comfortably fitted in are few. But chiefly, I suspect, it was my own unreadiness to offer more than a surface interest to strangers which left me so unusually isolated in this way, for other single women of my age often seem to lead more active social lives than I do.

I was not lonely because for many years I shared a flat with a cousin. My sister, who married during the war and went to live abroad soon after it, was less close to me than my cousin was and would not have been a more congenial companion, much as I liked her. Eight years younger than myself, my cousin was an exceptionally pretty girl with a haunting personality, so that her life was considerably fuller than mine, and I slid prematurely into an attitude common among good-natured middle-aged women: that of taking so strong an interest in other people's lives that it largely fills the emptiness of one's own. I was comfortable in the routine of those years, and when on rare occasions I felt a stab of misery my reaction to it was not revolt against my circumstances but a deliberate attempt to become resigned to them. But to say that satisfying work was something that had made me happy—that I could not have done. Something else, occupying only a fraction of each year and appearing to be marginal, made more difference to the colour of my days than did my work.

My holidays. I am not a traveller, only, once a year if I can manage it, a tourist. But those short journeys to France, Italy, Yugoslavia, or Greece have done more to alter my life than anything except love.

I owe them to the same aunt who taught me to enjoy painting. Before the war I had been taken abroad twice by my parents, driving fast round Europe on business trips, staying one night here, two nights there, never longer than the five or six nights we slept in Budapest. Most of each day was spent getting from place to place, and most of our meals were eaten with people to whom my father was selling mica, who were sometimes pleasant but rarely the companions we would have chosen. It was a useful bird's-eye view of Europe, but a frustrating one. We would be in Paris, Vienna, or Prague—places woven in my imagination from books, films, and hearsay into magical cities where anything might happen—and all that we would do was to go to bed early to be ready for an early start. I often had to share a room with my mother. I did not try to escape—my parents would not have allowed it, and I would have been scared—but I would long to lean out of the window into the foreign night, breathe the foreign smell of cigars, coffee, drains and unknown leaves, listen to the foreign dance music which always seemed to be coming so teasingly from lit doors and windows across the street. I wanted violently to be in these places, but with a man—with Paul, or with Robert, my Oxford love, or even with whatever man had been eyeing me across the room during dinner. Failing that, I wanted to sit by the window and write long letters to my friends describing my anguish. But I did not wish to hurt my parents by betraying how different I would have liked the journey to be, so I went to bed like a good girl, telling myself how lucky I was to be seeing these places (as indeed I was), and at breakfast the next morning I would be sulky.

Then, with the war, travel became impossible. I grew so accustomed to not thinking of it and to being short of money that I no longer saw it as something I could do. Given to inertia as I have always been, it is possible that if in 1947 my aunt had not unexpectedly sent me the money for a holiday abroad, I might never again have set foot on a Channel steamer.

It was a gift typical of her, offered shyly and suddenly, with no fuss. Can any other gift have bestowed so much pleasure? Without hesitation I plumped for Florence, and set off on that simple journey as tremulous with excitement as though I were crossing the Gobi desert. I expected to step out of the train into the gold, red, and blue of a painting by Fra Angelico, and shall never forget the shock of surprised recognition, the delicious anticipation-reality complex as I experienced it again on seeing that Florence was a crumbling biscuit baked pale by the sun, with a kind of beauty quite different from but much more disturbing than the beauty its name had held for me. I remembered Proust and his conjuring with names, his elaborate balancing of places not yet seen or no longer seen against places in their reality. 'That's not for me,' I thought. 'There's nothing to balance. This paving stone on which I am standing, that torn poster on that wall, that little dusty tree, that tomato skin in the gutter—any single object you like to name that I can see or touch is worth more to me than the whole of Petra or Angkor Vat in my imagination!'

Even more exciting than the discovery that Florence was real, was the discovery that the sudden distance between myself and my usual environment, the breaking of the daily habits by which I was conditioned, had released me from the creature produced by that conditioning. I felt as though I were my naked self, starting from scratch. A skin had been peeled off my eyes, my nerve-ends were exposed. I, who was usually able to sleep twelve or fourteen hours at a stretch if I were not woken, and would then get up reluctantly, found myself jumping out of bed at seven-thirty or eight in the morning, outraged by the idea that I should lie there one minute after my eyes had opened. There was no time to want anything but to be where I was and to see, see, see what I was seeing. That first turning loose after the war was the purest and most intense of all the holidays I have had, and it convinced me that from then on, whatever my circumstances, I must continue to travel abroad. It is not only seeing landscapes and works of art hitherto unseen, different kinds of building, faces of a different cast and complexion, behaviour formed in different moulds, which makes travelling important. It is the different eyes with which the traveller, startled out of habit by change, looks at these things.

To catalogue such ordinary journeys as mine would be tedious. I can put my finger on what I have gained from them by thinking of only one place from among those I have stayed in: the Greek island of Corfu, in the Ionian Sea.

I can recognize sandstone, chalk, and granite, but that is all. I cannot name the kind of rocks which lie under and jut through the thin skin of soil on Corfu, although the shapes of their abrupt and disorderly outcrops are printed on my brain. Hellenophiles sometimes refer to Corfu patronizingly as green and sóft, because it is so much less nakedly rocky than the Cyclades or most of the mainland, but in spite of its richness of vegetation its skeleton is almost as near the surface as that of the rest of Greece. It is rock, not earth. Its bones are not the sort that make smooth, swelling lines; they heave, break, and tumble, and their debris, from which the supporting walls of olive terraces are built, is rough, layered, pocked. The terraces are not hard to climb at any point because of the foot- and hand-holds offered by the crude masonry of the walls, but most of them have their 'paths': easy places made easier, where the rocks form steps or have been pressed by use into oblique, broken ledges where men climb regularly to the olive trees, and old women lead a goat or a donkey to be tethered on fresh grazing.

Each terrace has a different character. On some the stony earth, ochre or light terra-cotta, is almost bare, on others there are many thistles, among them a frail one of great beauty with steel-blue stems and leaves. On a recently grazed terrace the spiky grasses and small flowers will be flattened and scattered with dung, drying quickly into earthiness, while another will be green, with a higher percentage of what the English recognize as grass in its growth, and softer, more caressing plants. Each terrace has its tree or trees, with a slight depression round the roots to hold the rain when it comes.

I am a connoisseur of terraces. I look for one greener and therefore softer than the rest, with the best view possible and an old, well-grown tree to throw a wider and more opaque shade than a young tree can. Such a tree is easy to find on Corfu, where the method of cultivation (due, say other Greeks, to Corfiot laziness) is to leave olives alone and let them grow to a great age and size until they split and gnarl into extraordinary shapes. Their trunks become distorted, ropelike columns of bark-enclosed tendons which writhe apart, then join again, sometimes leaving windows of space so that you can look right through the tree. They give an impression of restless movement curiously at variance with their gentle, peaceful colouring. I have seen dull olive trees in France, Italy, and some parts of Greece—little orchard trees, monotonous in shape and no more than pretty—but because of those on Corfu, the olive is the tree I would choose to keep if I could have only one: for the variety of shape, for the comforting roughness of its bark, for its minnow leaves, dark on top and silver underneath, which cast a shadow more delicately stippled than any other, and for its ancient usefulness, which makes it, like wheat, a symbolic thing.

There is one terrace at Paleokastritsa, on the west side of Corfu, which I first found six years ago and revisited last year. Its position favours the holding of moisture and it is almost meadowlike compared to its neighbours. It is possible, though not particularly comfortable, to lie on it without spreading a rug or a towel against prickles. (One gets better at lying as the days pass. At first every pebble and spike and exploring ant is a discomfort; but after several

days of sun and wine and oil one's body relaxes and becomes accommodating, so that one could almost sleep as Greek workmen sleep in
the heat of the afternoon, lying loose and comfortable on roadside
stones.)

Although this terrace would be a good place for sleeping, I have
never slept on it because I found it impossible to stop looking.
Below it, only a little masked by the silver tops of lower trees,
is one of the bays of Paleokastritsa. This is a place where land
and sea meet in an interlocking clover-leaf formation, three almost
enclosed bays divided from each other by two steep promontories which may once have been islands, since they are joined to
the steeper main island by a narrow strip of flat land. One of the
promontories is crowned by a small monastery, but the one on
which my terrace is has only rebarbative scrub and rock above its
orchards. The best-known bay is under the monastery, round and
dark blue, with a small hotel on its beach. The bay I overlooked
is bigger, less regular in shape and more beautiful in colour. It
is broken by a small promontory within it, and goes from navy
blue near the open sea, through every shade of aquamarine, with
depths of pure emerald under its cliffs and chunky emerald patches
where a boat throws a shadow. Its depth and the nature of its sandy
bottom combine in a ratio perfect for transparency, sparkle, and
movement—I have never seen it when it was not netted with light,
whereas some Mediterranean and Aegean bays, though lovely, can
become almost too still, too smooth. Only to look at this bay is
like drinking champagne would be if I enjoyed champagne, and
to swim in it is something quite different from swimming in any
other water that I know. From where I sat I looked back across it
at the mainland. Just under the terrace is the strip of beach which

edges the flat, linking neck, with a tiny, shacklike taverna, a few caïques and rowing-boats lying at anchor, where one or two fishermen, either old men or very young boys, move slowly about and sometimes call to each other. Beyond that, cliffs (at the bottom of one of them a little spring of fresh water bubbles up a few inches from the sea—one of the several places where Ulysses is supposed to have been found by Nausicaa, although there is no room for the bushes or reeds in which he hid his nakedness); above the cliffs steep, olive-fleeced, cypress-punctuated mountainside, rising to an abrupt escarpment with a sheer rock-face which turns apricot-coloured in the evening sun and is rimmed by the rapid, stumbling line of the mountain's profile, plunging out and round to one's right to hit the sea on the far side of the bay.

All this is bathed in light and silence. It is silent in spite of the fishermen's voices or the occasional grinding of a truck or taxi creeping round the edge of the bay to visit the hotel or the monastery; silent in spite of a donkey on a lower terrace calling to another donkey on the further mountain. The braying of donkeys—that painful, wheezing, lionlike sound—might be the voice of rock, as the creaking of cicadas might be the voice of sun. I once spent four hours alone on that terrace with an unread book and untouched writing-pad, turned by the spectacle into nothing but eyes, with no idea of the time that was passing until the sun went down.

Such pleasures can only be enjoyed alone and on foot. Earth, stone, water, trees must be touched and smelt in order to be fully realized. I have seen landscapes more magnificent from cars, buses, trains, and boats, and have been pleased to see them; but the ones I have *learnt,* the ones which have become part of the fabric of my memory, are those which have made the muscles of my legs ache, have scratched my ankles and caused sweat to drip off my forehead. Why I should still consider the conscientious hiker slightly absurd I cannot conceive. He is undoubtedly gaining a more intense and enduring experience than any other traveller.

A small, slow motor bicycle would be a good substitute for walking. I have been taken across Corfu from Paleokastritsa to the town of Corfu itself, a distance of just over twenty miles, riding pillion on such a machine, and a thousand nuances of a road which I thought I knew well became evident, its smells especially. The smells released in a Mediterranean climate by evening, when the baked herbs and aromatic leaves begin to breathe again, are almost as positive as clouds of colour, but only wisps of them can be caught from a car. I was riding behind the sedate manager of the hotel at Paleokastritsa, who liked a speed of about fifteen miles an hour: perfect in the circumstances. The friend who was with me was piloted by one of the waiters on a racier scooter, and would have been hurtled across the island like a thunderbolt had the manager and I not started out first and the waiter felt that it would be *lèse-majesté* to overtake his employer. So through the golden evening we trundled, weaving among the potholes to a dialogue of 'pip-pip,' 'beep-beep,' whenever we had to pass a donkey with a load of brushwood, or half a dozen thin sheep. It would, I thought, have been the ideal way to travel about Greece.

The hurtling came later, at one o'clock in the morning, when we were on our way back by taxi from the dinner to which we had been invited. In England a car or a restaurant with a radio in it depresses me. Had I been told of a taxi with not only a radio but a gramophone, I should have been appalled. How could one bear to drive through an arcadian landscape untouched by time, under a full moon at that, to the sound of rock-and-roll or even of bouzoukia? But given an evening drinking retsina with a soap manufacturer and a municipal electrician in Corfu, those great gales of sound became exhilarating. The taxi bounced, the moon reeled, scented breezes whipped our hair, the two men sang in passionate baritone voices and embraced us, and although the fierce, tomcat wailing of the Greek music was the better, even the Elvis Presley records played in our honour took on a throb and a swing which fitted them to the night. Only on Corfu have I seen taxis fitted with that device: a narrow, cushioned slot on gimbals under the dashboard, into which the driver shoves small records from the library which he keeps on the seat beside him. He only has to push them in and pull them out; the playing is automatic and undisturbed by even the most violent bouncing. Loud it has to be—loud and strident, with the hood of the car down and a road diversified by sharp bends and sudden stretches of unsurfaced stone. Then the music becomes not an offence but a celebration, one hears it as its addicts hear it, vulgarity is blown away, and its platitudes touch the nerves like truths.

Strenuous though the end of such an evening usually is, streaked with anxiety as to how to taper stormy declarations of premature and unreal passion into an agreeable acquaintanceship, I would not have missed the wild musical taxis of Corfu. Evenings like that—absurd, comic, undignified, even at times slightly alarming—following days like those I spent on the terrace: those are what I travel for. That I should see works of arts and monuments which I should not see otherwise, and that I should make the sudden but enduring friendships which sometimes blossom out of a time when inhibitions are melted by strangeness and renewed vitality, is certainly important; but the secret days and the comic evenings have been the best treasure I have brought back.

Anglo-Saxon and Scandinavian women are commonly supposed to go south in search of men, and so they often do. The neuroses of northern societies, in which men feel that they see too much of women, dovetail neatly with those of southern societies, where men feel that they see too little of them. Whether she shrinks or expands under it, no Englishwoman can remain unaware of having her sex openly recognized in street, train, or restaurant, after months at home during which the most startling recognition it has received has been the quick, sidelong twitch of a gooseberry eye here and there, which vanishes under a hat brim as soon as it has been observed. Whatever the weather, I feel cold when I return to London.

But societies which acknowledge the power of sex, and therefore shelter their respectable women (and thereby increase the power of sex—it is a spiral), are romanticized by societies with opposite tendencies. Much nonsense is talked by swaggering southerners and wistful northerners about the absence of puritanism and inhibition in the warmer parts of Europe. So much theorizing, so much emphasis on masculine *bella figura,* so much keeping of scores—it is not, perhaps, repressed sex that one encounters in countries like Italy and Greece, but it sometimes looks suspiciously like sex-in-the-head. And in spite of the millions of real and warm relationships that must exist, fat Yanni Hajikakkis, admittedly an extreme case, seems to me to have his significance.

He was a huge, thick-necked man with a bellow, who boasted that during his military service he had been the most spectacular sergeant in the Greek Army, able to make even colonels jump out of their boots when he let himself go. In ordinary conversation he would try to keep his voice down, but he never succeeded for more than a few sentences. Swimming with a friend of mine, at whom he was making a desultory pass, he could be heard across fifty yards of water and the beach, from the balconies of the small hotel which stood on its edge, as he argued, 'But you cannot like to make love with your husband or you would not be here without him.' In the Army he had been popular because he had never put his men in prison but had taken offenders outside and punched their heads, which, he told us, had made him much loved. Yanni was on holiday in Corfu when we met him, a prosperous store-owner from Salonika, rich, and contented with his lot except in one way. His mother was dead. His father was dead too, 'but for my father I am not suffering. For Mama . . . "Not Mama!" I say, "No, God, not my Mama, not my Mama!" But God did not hear. . . . What is a man without his mother? In a man's life she is his angel, she is the only pure love. I make love to many women—I am a strong man as you see, I am always making love—but what are these whores to me? I love only my Mama and she loves only me, she would die for me—and now she is dead!'

Whenever Yanni spoke of his mama's death, and he spoke of it every time I met him, his big bold eyes would pop with tears, he would bow his head and drop his fists on the table so that the glasses rattled. Large, loud, and aggressively masculine though he was, through my head there would flash images of thousands of plump, soft, pale little boys—cherished, indulged little Greek boys of the middle and upper classes—growing up in a society which inspires western Europeans with nostalgia because its values are simpler and more ancient than our own, because its members believe that children love mothers, that brothers protect sisters, that insults should be revenged, and that something has been lost since they can no longer shoot their enemies without getting into trouble. No doubt there are some little Greek boys of that kind whose value as children and males in such a society does not mean that sweetmeats are stuffed between their lips even when they do not ask for them, or who are not allowed to stay up long past their bedtime because they cry and kick, but they are the minority. Mostly the baby, and particularly the boy baby, is god, and that this privileged status makes the best sort of man of him can appear doubtful.

'Now that you are so lonely,' I said to Yanni, 'why don't you get married?'

'Married? I will never marry! How can I find today such a girl as I would marry?'

What qualities would he require, I asked, and he catalogued them: she need not be rich because he was rich, and he held opinions too modern for him to insist on money as a matter of form; she need not be pretty, though it would be better if she were; she must come from a suitable family; she must be no more than seventeen so that he could be sure that she was a virgin (in England, he said, she would have to be under fifteen for that, from all he had heard). But above all 'she must be like my mother, she must be to me a mama.' It was distressing to think that this prosperous man, still only in his thirties, almost certainly would get married soon in spite of his protests: that some girl in her teens really *would* have to buckle down to being his mama because he felt in his bones that mamas were the only kind of women who were good. Englishmen are supposed to be split-minded about women, to divide them into 'good' and 'bad' according to whether they like men or not, but no Englishman I have ever met was more split-minded than poor fat Yanni, slumped over a café table and bellowing the loss of his mother like a calf bereft.

Some western Europeans go to Greece—I go to Greece—not only for its haunting beauty but to touch a life more straightforward and governed by simpler necessities than our own. After being spellbound by it we turn back to our own values and see them as overcomplex, shoddy, and absurd—I have found myself envying Greek or Yugoslav women for their unquestioning acceptance of their status in a world more dominated by men than my own. But not when I was talking to Yanni; and not when, for example, I have ventured into a Greek restaurant at night in a provincial town—a restaurant kept as a preserve for men, by men, because men believe that it is right to keep their mothers, daughters, and sisters safely at home behind invisible bars. If there is a woman entertainer in the restaurant, singing bouzoukia, watch those hungry faces turned towards her, listen to the groan which greets her demure and lazy dancing—the pressure of frustration is explosive. The woman tourist who fondly believes herself to be succumbing to an uninhibited pagan is more likely to be serving as a crust thrown to a starving man—a deliberately starving man, who would only pick up a crust because a crust is worth nothing. If all she wants is to be free of her own inhibitions for a day or two, well and good, but I suspect that the freedom is often bestowed by someone no less cramped than herself.

Having too little money is an advantage in travelling which I regret losing. I am still far from being able to stay in really good hotels or to fly except on the cheaper night flights, but my standards are creeping up: cheap the flight may be, but it is a flight, and not a third-class train journey. It would be possible to travel more cheaply than necessity dictates, but fondly though I remember journeys made in less comfort, I feel myself reflecting a miniature image of the rich whose money forces them so inexorably into a certain manner of living. It seems an affectation not to take a room with a shower if I can afford it, although I know by experience that a hotel too small for showers will be less impersonal. I *know* that an excursion by local bus is more amusing and interesting than an excursion by taxi, in spite of the heat, the jolting, and the passenger who will vomit, but the money in my purse works a sinister distortion, emphasizing the bus's disadvantages, highlighting the taxi's luxury, so that against my will I find myself in the latter, and thus likely to meet other people of my own sort instead of the friendly, curious strangers in the bus. An insulating layer has been put between my naked self and the place I am visiting, and I have lost something by it. I can only be grateful that the layer is never likely to become thick.

From every journey I have made I have come home happier, and what I have gained from them has not vanished with time. It is not only that I have seen beautiful things with which to furnish my imagination, learnt interesting things, met interesting people, laughed a great deal. Something has happened as a result of all this: one by one, nerves which I thought to be dead have come to life.

16

B Y 1958, WHEN I was forty-one, I had come to feel that middle-age, provided I did not look more than a little way ahead, was a peaceful time rather than a depressing one. A deliberate myopia could give the impression that I was on a level plain rather than on a downhill slope. It was a long time since I had been in love, a long time since every unoccupied moment had been filled with thoughts of men, or of a man. Sometimes, when I went to bed, I would try to return to the memories, hopes, speculations, and dreams which had taken up so much of my time for so many years, but I would fall asleep before they had properly begun. I worked, and liked my job. I travelled, and loved it. I met my friends, and was as familiar with their troubles as though they were my own; and because trouble was the prevailing condition in the life of almost everyone I knew, my own calm, though negative, began to seem a good fortune. My grandmother had died, and soon afterwards my father, who had retired some years earlier and had been living with my mother in a house they had bought near Beckton during the war, when it had become necessary for the Farm to house a working bailiff. These deaths, and the ageing of my other relatives, who were shrinking a little and stiffening in their joints, while their loneliness and their fear of it showed through the chinks in their courage as they pushed their days so bravely from incident to incident, had put Beckton in a new light—or had made me notice the new light sharply for the first time. It was no longer a place to which I could go back for comfort; it had become a place to which I ought to bring comfort, and the meagreness with which I did this made me realize the degree to which I had become detached from my family. When I spent a weekend with my mother I could talk only of her affairs, or of the most superficial of my own, because on many of the subjects which touched me closely our opinions and emotions would be too different for easy communication.

Or so I felt, and continue to feel with people of her generation and background. I wish, now, that in my youth I had loved my family less. If I had not loved them I might have had the courage for revolt, instead of going quietly underground. If in my twenties I had been open about the sexual freedom I was practising, had pressed political arguments instead of sliding out of them into silence, had discussed my agnosticism instead of merely avoiding going to church, there might not have been the breach I expected and feared—or, if there had been, it might not have been permanent. With divergencies openly recognized it might have become possible for us to touch at more than a few well-defined points. Instead, I find myself apparently permanently inhibited in such relationships, even to keeping almost entirely silent on the most important thing that has ever happened to me.

For one January morning in 1958 I was crossing the Outer Circle in Regent's Park, bringing my dog in from her walk, when a passing car slowed, accelerated again, slowed and stopped. Supposing that the driver wanted to ask the way somewhere, I turned towards the car. The man peering back at me over his shoulder looked familiar. 'Why, it's Marcel!' I thought. Marcel was a diamond-polisher from Johannesburg whom I had once known well. I began to hurry towards him, smiling, but when I got nearer I saw that it was not Marcel. 'The name is Mustafa Ali from Istanbul,' said the stranger. 'I was wondering whether you would have a cup of coffee with me.'

I explained that I had mistaken him for someone else, told him I was busy, and crossed the road, laughing. 'What optimism,' I thought, 'at nine o'clock in the morning! And how odd that someone looking so like Marcel should do such a Marcellish thing.' I began to remember Marcel. For the rest of the day I felt extraordinarily alive and cheerful, and that evening, as soon as I got home, I began to write about Marcel.

It went smoothly for several pages—the little man was there in front of me, I got him down—but when, next day, I reread what I had done, it was clear that I could not persuade what I had written into any shape. Marcel would have to belong to a story about diamonds, and I did not know enough about the trade. 'Well, it was rather fun remembering him,' I thought, putting it aside, but the energy, the feeling of something bubbling inside me, was still there. I went on thinking about him until he reminded me of another man whom I had once known for a short time, and at that point it happened. 'By God,' I thought with jubilation, 'I know what I'll do: I'll write about *him,* and I'm going to get it *just as it was.*' That story came straight out, with no pause, exactly as I meant it to, and I was perfectly happy all the time it was coming.

Until I left school I had written poems fairly regularly. I wrote half a dozen more while I was at Oxford, and another three or four, widely spaced, when I was in my twenties. They were not good and I did not suppose them to be good, but they were real in the sense that they were pushed out of me by their own growth rather than pulled out by my volition. They represented intensities of experience, they were high points of my 'real' life, but they were secret. I did not think of myself as someone whose intensities deserved to be communicated, so when they stopped coming I was regretful but not distressed.

Writing prose was something of which I had rarely thought except as an enviable gift possessed by others. Two or three times, when more than usually short of money, I had taken some incident and tried to turn it into a 'travel piece' for the *New Statesman* or a 'funny piece' for *Punch,* without success. I was facetious when I tried to be funny, high-flown when I tried to describe. I could see clearly enough that I would dislike the results if they had been produced by someone else. Three times during my adult life I had scribbled a few pages for no purpose other than to put down what I was feeling: once about Crivelli's *Annunciation,* once about Forster's *A Passage to India,* and once about my first visit to Florence. These I kept, but simply as reminders to myself. The 'feel' of the story triggered by Mr Mustafa Ali was entirely different. I did not bother to envisage a market for it, but it was, from the beginning, a story which I meant people to read.

As soon as that story was finished, another one began, and by the end of the year I had written nine. I did not think about them in advance: a feeling would brew up, a first sentence would occur to me, and then the story would come, as though it had been there all the time. Sometimes it would turn into 'work' halfway through and I would have to cast about for the conclusion to which the story must be brought, but more often it finished itself. Some of them connected very closely with my own experience, some of them, to my astonishment, depended on it so slightly that they might almost have been 'invented' (the 'invented' ones were the ones of which I felt most proud, although, with one exception, the others were better).

In March, when I was halfway through the third of these stories, I saw the announcement of the *Observer's* short-story competition for that year, the story to be called 'The Return' and to be three thousand words long. Neither of my finished stories had that title, but it could have made sense with either of them. One was too long, the other only needed cutting by a hundred words. Friends had encouraged me, so I put the shorter of the two in an envelope, chose for the necessary pseudonym the name of the horse which had just won the Grand National (Mr What, God bless him), posted it and forgot it. Or rather, I remembered it twice between then and December, when the results were to be announced, on selling two other stories to magazines. 'Perhaps,' I thought, 'if these have proved good enough to sell. . . . ' But both times I slapped myself down so firmly that when the literary editor of the *Observer* telephoned me at my office on December 21st, my birthday, the competition did not enter my head.

I had written to him a little earlier, asking him whether his paper had omitted to review one of our books because he did not like it, or because he had lost it—the sort of nagging a publisher only permits himself for a book he cares about. I was therefore pleased to hear that he was on the line, and more pleased when he said that he had good news for me. 'Hurrah,' I thought. 'He is going to send it out for review after all.'

'At least, I think I have good news,' he went on, 'if it *is* for you. . . . Did you send in a story for our competition?'

The consolation prizes, I thought in a split second. There were several of them, of twenty-five pounds each. 'Yes,' I said.

'Then you have won first prize,' he said. 'You have won five hundred pounds.'

You do not look up because you know that you cannot climb the tree. You have forgotten, by now, that there is fruit hidden among its leaves. Then, suddenly, without a puff of wind, a great velvety peach falls plump into your hand. It happens to other people, perhaps; it never happens to oneself. . . . I am still licking peach juice off my fingers.

Although, if the metaphor is to be exact, the peach does not fall into your hand so much as land on your head. It stuns you. Imagining such an event, I would have imagined blank incredulity followed by a clean burst of rapture, but the two emotions blurred together, there was no perfect moment. By the time I had gathered my wits to accept such a moment, I found that it was already in the past, I had had it. Something ought to *happen* at moments of delicious surprise: one ought to fly up into the air, one ought to change into music or light. I went on sitting at my desk, watching the cold pigeons huddling on a bit of roof outside my office window, and it was totally inadequate. Even when I was hurrying down Bond Street at lunch-time that day, buying prettier Christmas presents than I had planned, I found that frustration was mixed with my delight because none of the people in the street looked as though the world had changed. There were moments during that lovely day when I felt that I had better stop groping or I might touch a thread of real anguish in the evanescence of moments. For the first time in years I remembered little Rosalba's song from *The Rose and the Ring,* and I was humming it all day:

> *Oh what fun*
> *To have a plum bun,*
> *How I wish*
> *It never were done!*

But although at first it seemed as though nothing—or not enough—had changed, two things did happen as a result of this event: one of them no more than an amusing insight, the other with a value hard to calculate.

'Poverty' is a word which should be forbidden to anyone who has lived as comfortably as I have lived, with a family in the background which, however ill it could afford it, could be counted on to rescue me in an emergency. But I have never had any income beyond my earnings, and my earnings have always been small. (The small independent publisher who does not plough most of his profits back into his firm will soon either dwindle to nothing, or stop being independent.) Every penny I have earned I have always spent at once, and always without having many of the things I would have liked. To me, therefore, five hundred pounds tax-free seemed wealth. I could go to Greece during the coming spring without worrying—I could even travel *first-class!* I could buy a fitted carpet, and new curtains which I really liked, and there would still be money over. During that winter I felt rich, and because I felt it I gave an impression of being it. A little while earlier I had been looking at dresses in a large, smart shop, and when I had pointed to a pretty one and said 'I'll try that,' the girl serving me had answered in a tired voice: 'It's expensive. Why try on something you can't afford?' In the same shop, wearing the same clothes, soon after I had paid my five hundred pounds into the bank, I was served with such civil alacrity that I could have ordered two grand pianos to be sent home on approval and they would have offered a third. Courteous men spent hours unrolling bolts of material for me, urging me to consider another, and yet another. A pattern for matching? Why, yes! And instead of the strip two inches wide which I was expecting, lengths big enough to make a bedspread were procured for me. For about a month I believe I could have furnished a whole house on credit, not because I was looking different, not because I could, in fact, afford it; simply because, for the first time in my life and for no very solid reason, I was feeling carefree about money. I learnt a great deal about the power of mood during that month.

The second happening was of more consequence. This plenty was the result of competent judges preferring my story to several thousand others, and my story was something I had done spontaneously, for the pleasure of it; something as much a part of me as the colour of my eyes. To have written one story considered good does not amount to much, but it does amount to something: it is not failure. It would be an absurd exaggeration to say that for twenty years I had been unhappy—I had enjoyed many things, and for most of the later years I had been contented enough—but it is the exact truth to say that if, at any minute during those years I had been asked to think about it, made to stop doing whatever was distracting me and pass judgment on my own life, I should have said without hesitation that failure was its essence. I had never really wanted anything but the most commonplace satisfactions of a woman's life, and those, which I had wanted passionately, I had failed to achieve. That I would have answered in such a way is not speculation. I *did* answer exactly that, to myself, over and over again, in the minutes before falling asleep, in the worse minutes of waking up, when I was walking down a street, when I looked up from a book, while I was stirring scrambled eggs in a pan. The knowledge was my familiar companion. It had been, at first, hot coals of pain and grief, and had later grown cold; but cold though it had become, its lumpy presence had still been there. My only pride had been that having by nature an easy disposition, and a fund of pleasure in life stored up from a happy childhood and youth, I was good at living with failure. I did not think that it had turned me disagreeable or mad, and that I considered an achievement.

And now something which did not go against my grain, something which was as natural to me as love, had worked. I believe that even had I never written another word, the success of that story alone would have begun to dissolve the lumps. Bury me, dear friends, with a copy of the *Observer* folded under my head, for it was the *Observer's* prize that woke me up to the fact that I had become happy.

It is surely important to make a few notes on that rare condition, happiness, now that I am in it. It began when I started to write, was fanned into a glorious glow when I won that prize, was confirmed when, soon afterwards, I began to love, and it shows no sign of altering.

A symptom of life: opening my eyes in the morning to wakefulness.

The long hours of unconsciousness which I used to treasure are now meaningless. Even on Sundays I will sleep for no more than eight hours unless I am unusually and genuinely tired.

A symptom of life: not caring much where I live. Single women can root themselves in their rooms, their furniture, their ornaments, so that not to have the right things about them in the right order becomes intolerable to them. I love rooms and objects and materials; I love to choose them and to arrange them, and when—rarely—I have done it well, I am snug and satisfied. But I attach less importance to it now than I used to. Recently, being between flats, I have been camping here and there with friends, and once in a place which was everything I dislike. I expected to be uneasy and discontented, but found that while there was a table to write on, a stove to cook on, and a bed, I was at home.

A symptom of life: people saying 'What has happened to her? She looks so well,' or 'She looks so young.' My own sensation of physical well-being is perceptible to other people. 'She might be twenty-five,' said a woman in her seventies, and even allowing for the telescoping of the years when seen from that age, which would make thirty-five more accurate than twenty-five, some degree of physical rejuvenation is suggested. If it exists, it corresponds to an inward change towards the years. I was twenty-three when I began to be aware of ageing as something sad. While I had Paul every year passing carried me towards something better than I had hitherto known, possibilities proliferated, anything might happen to me. When I had accepted his disappearance the years became slow steps downhill. Common sense forbade me to consider myself old while still in my twenties, but I felt old, and once past my thirtieth birthday I began to accept the feeling as rational. Most of my thirties were overshadowed, when I allowed myself to notice it, not only by my forties but by my old age: by a sense that there was nothing ahead but old age, by an awareness of the disabilities of old age, a shrinking when I watched an old person stepping carefully, painfully on to the curb of a pavement, or noticed the round, puzzled eyes of old-age pensioners sitting on a bench in the sun, looking baffled by what had happened to them. Now that I am, in fact, several years nearer to them, have my first grey hairs, a neck less smooth and a waist considerably less slim—can observe in my own body the clear indications of time passing and know that they are there for good, not as a sign of a physical condition that could be cured—I have, perversely, stopped feeling old. The process of ageing is undeniable, but it no longer touches an exposed nerve. Being happy has made it unimportant.

This is because the present has become real. No one can be detached from his past, but anyone can come to see it as being past, and when that happens one is partly liberated from its consequences. I cannot only see mine as being past, but have become indifferent to it. *Then* is less real than *now,* and *now* has become potent enough to shape the future, who knows how, so that the future is no longer an immutable threat. Nothing is immutable: that is the thing. My condition has changed—even, to a small extent, my nature has changed—so possibilities exist again.

The sensation of happiness itself is one for which I have only a physical vocabulary: warmth, expansion, floating, opening, relaxation. This was so from its beginning, and has become more so with its confirmation in love. Unintellectual, unspiritual as I am, I have always identified closely with my body: for most of the time I am it and it is me. What happens to me physically is therefore of great importance to my general condition—a disposition threatening serious problems in illness or old age, but conducive to an especial happiness in love. To split the relationship of love into 'physical' and 'mental' is something which I cannot do. Making love is not a fugitive good, contained only in the time in which it is being done: it is, each time, an addition, an expansion of a whole happiness. I have never in the past known it to be quite wiped out by subsequent events, and I know that it will not be wiped out now. This final way of communication is one of the things which, like my feeling for Beckton and Oxford, I know to be stored in me: a *good* which I have experienced, which enters into and is entered by everything I see and hear and feel and smell, and of which I can only be deprived by the decay of consciousness. That when two people have lived together for several years their love-making loses its value is, in most cases, obvious, and I should expect it to do so with me: I should expect that only if the man I was living with and I were really as well suited as we had first believed would the habit of companionship and inter-dependence successfully supersede physical delight. But I do not see that this would discredit physical delight. If it exists, it will always *have existed.* Now, therefore, that it exists again for me, I am by that much richer to the end of my days.

So happiness, followed by love and increased by it, has for me the colour of physical pleasure although it embraces many other things and although it seems to me to mean something larger than my own emotions and sensations. This is a period in which many people are concerned with the difficulty of communication. Poetry, novels, plays, paintings: they emphasize this theme so constantly that anyone who feels that human beings *can* communicate is beginning to look naïve. But what is meeting a man from a different country, a different tradi-tion, a different social and economic background, and finding that you and he can both speak about anything exactly as you feel, in perfect confidence of understanding even if not of agreement, if it is not communication? The discovery of trust and easiness which comes with such a meeting is another, and greater, enduring good.

On the face of it this love is of the same kind as others I have known and is no more likely to lead to a permanent companionship. I must take my own word for it that it is not the same. It does not feel the same. *Then,* with a sort of despairing joy, I used to jump off cliffs into expected disaster; *now,* hardly knowing what I was doing, I slipped off a smooth rock into clear, warm water.

I have come to have a horror of many of the states to which human beings give the name of love—a horror at the sight of them, and at the knowledge that I have been in them. I feel like André Gide, when he wrote in *So Be It,* 'There are many sufferings I claim to be imaginary . . . few things interest me less than so-called broken hearts and sentimental affairs.' Gide, poor man, was not well equipped to talk about love, split as he knew himself to be between physical and mental to such an extent that both were crippled. (I know of no more striking example of the dependence of style on honesty than his descriptions of relationships with boys. Trying to write most honestly, he is betrayed by the sudden, tinny ring of his words because he is not writing honestly. He is persuading himself that a sick greed had beauty. I would have been prepared to believe that it *did* have beauty if it were not for the timbre of those sentences.) But the old man's impatience with sad love stories contains much truth. Hunger, possessiveness, self-pity, the stubborn obsession to impose on another being the image we ourselves have fabricated: good God, the torments human beings are impelled to inflict on themselves and each other!

I am frightened by my own arrogance in saying that now, because I had stopped expecting to love and had therefore almost stopped wanting to love, I love; but that is what it feels like. I do not want the man I love to be other than he is; I want more of his time and presence than he is free to give me, but not much more. I want him to exist as himself, without misfortune or unhappiness. Perhaps this is because I am too old and fixed in my habits to want anything more, or perhaps I am deceiving myself. If I am telling the truth—I must reread this in ten years' time!—I shall have been justified in calling my present condition happiness.

I do not think that I have become more agreeable for it. My relationship with other people has changed: they have, with one exception, become less important to me. In a sad or neutral condition I pored over my friends' lives almost to the extent of living them vicariously, whereas now I am more detached, particularly from their misfortunes. I have one friend, a woman, who is bound by some flaw in her nature to uncertainty and confusion so that she has rarely been able to know the rewards which her beauty, intelligence, and generous ways ought to have earned her. There have been times in the past when I was so concerned for her that I would lie awake puzzling her problems in real distress, but now, although I am still sorry for them, they no longer attack my own peace of mind. This increased selfishness both dismays and pleases me: dismays, because it is disagreeable to see in oneself so clear a demonstration of the limitations of sympathy; pleases, because I have suspected the motives of the concern I used to feel. A fictional character who has always made me uneasy is Sonia, in *War and Peace*—humble, unselfish Sonia, abdicating from her own claims on life, identifying so thoroughly with the Rostovs that their lives were substituted for hers. Tolstoy need do no more than present Sonia without comment to show that in spite of her virtues he dismisses her as a person incomplete, a failed human being. His attitude towards her has always made me wince: it is the right attitude, and there have been times when I myself was near deserving it. To grasp greedily is detestable; to abdicate is despicable. When unhappy, I have veered towards the despicable rather than the detestable, and if vanity must choose between the two evils, whose vanity would not prefer to be detested rather than despised?

In these circumstances happiness will, of course, end, in so far as it depends on a relationship. Or if not 'of course,' then 'probably.' I have been puzzled because, in foreseeing this probability, I remain sure that I am not 'expecting disaster' as I used to do when I fell in love. If the man I love were to stop loving me, or were to go away, there would certainly be an eclipse of joy at first total: I should have a bad time to go through. Am I so far from being frightened by this only because I can see no reason why such a thing should happen *soon?* Is it because, growing old, I am used to the thought of the losses which come with age, so that I would see such a loss as just another of them? Or is it because I happen to trust the relationship as one in which no mystification is likely to enter (the worst part of Paul's disappearance was the silence)? No doubt these things contribute to my lack of 'disaster-expectation,' but there is something else as well. It is embarrassing to revert to my writing when it still amounts to so little—to hardly more than a private satisfaction—but I believe that it is the impulse to write which underlies my peace of mind. If I ask myself, 'So what will become of me if *that* happens?' the answer is, 'I will be all right after a time. I will go on writing.' And because I can say that, I can live in the present with nothing but gratitude for and joy in what it offers.

It is now midnight, early in December. From this table, with this white tea-cup, full ashtray, and small glass half-full of rum beside me, I see my story, ordinary though it has all been and sad though much of it was, as a success story. I am rising forty-three, and I am happier in the present and more interested by the future than I have ever been since I was a girl: amused and delighted, too, because to find oneself in the middle of a success story, however modest, when one has for so long believed oneself a protagonist of failure, is bizarre. But is it a story which will seem worth having lived through, of value in itself, when I come to die? Will the question my grandmother asked—and I shall have no grandchild of whom to ask it—overshadow my last days?

17

THE THINGS WHICH I will not be able to claim for myself are easy to list.

I have not been beautiful. Looks do not matter, I was taught; indeed, handsome looks are even bad, tempting to vanity and silliness. This, for a woman, is a lie. If I had been beautiful I would not necessarily have been happier, but I would have been more important. Perhaps if I had been ugly I would also have been more important, an awkward body forced to build an awkward personality to protect grief. But my kind of looks—someone may say, surprised, 'How pretty you look in that colour,' or, if in love with me, 'You have lovely eyes'—that kind of looks cannot be accounted even momentarily a reason for existence, as beauty, so confusingly and sometimes so fatally, can be.

I have been intelligent only in comparison with dull people. Compared with what I consider real intelligence I am stupid, being unable to think. I do not even know what people do in their brains to start the process of thinking. My own brain has a door which swings backwards and forwards in the draught. Things blow into it—a lot of things, some of them good but none of them under my control as I feel they ought to be. I have intuitions, sympathies, a sense of proportion, and the ability to be detached, but nothing which goes click-click-click, creating structures of thought. In my work I am often humiliated by this inability to think. I do things, or leave them undone, purely through stupidity, and this hurts and puzzles me, so that each time it happens I turn quickly to something unconnected with the organization of facts or ideas. I am good at liking or not liking somebody's work or, at understanding what somebody means, or is trying to mean. If I am wrong about such things, it is for reasons other than stupidity. But because I see the ability to organize and to construct as something which it should be possible to learn, and I have not been able to learn it, I am more oppressed, in my work, by my lack than I am comforted by what I have. Outside work, in life, I do not mind being stupid in this way; it is sometimes inconvenient but that is my own business, and I get pleasure and interest enough from the blowing about of feelings. But clearly I shall not be able to claim intelligence of a high enough quality to justify a life.

I have not been good. My 'good,' partly a legacy of my Christian upbringing and partly arrived at empirically, is one which centres on selflessness. I have seen few evils, and few ills, which could not be traced to the individual's monstrous misconceptions of his own value in relation to that of other individuals. But people are what they *do* more than what they believe; and over and over again my actions have been those of a woman who values things as trivial as her own comfort or convenience above another person's joy or sorrow.

I have not been brave or energetic. To push back the frontiers of experience is an activity which I believe to be essential, but lethargy and timidity have prevented my doing it to anything like the extent to which it would have been possible. For political engagement I have been too lazy; for exploratory travel I have been too unenterprising, fearing the insecurity in strange places which it would entail for someone with no money. My sympathies are with the hipster, but when I consider his techniques of broadening experience I can see myself in comparison, as square as a cube from a child's set of bricks: to me excesses bring discomfort and fatigue rather than freedom.

So I have not been beautiful, or intelligent, or good, or brave, or energetic, and for many years I was not happy: I failed to achieve the extremely simple things which, for so long, I wanted above all else: I found no husband and it is not likely that I shall ever have a child.

There is plenty of evidence, then, that my existence has been without value: that if, like my grandmother, I approach death slowly and consciously, I shall be driven to ask the question she asked: 'What have I lived for?' All that I shall be able to answer is that I have written a little, and I have loved, and if I do not die until I am old, those things will have become too remote to count for much. I shall remember that they once seemed worth everything, but quite possibly the fact that by then they will be *over* will appear to have wiped out their value. It ought to be a frightening thought, but I am still not frightened.

I was looking through a dictionary of quotations in search of a title for a friend's play when I chanced on Carlyle and Ruskin, both saying something which caught my attention. Carlyle: 'No most gifted eye can exhaust the significance of any object.' Ruskin: 'The greatest thing a human soul does in this world is to see.'

Eyes are precarious little mechanisms, lodged in their sockets as though that were that. When I was living at Beckton we used to buy the heads of sheep for our dogs, boil them, then strip or gouge the meat from them. It was a horrifying job until you became used to it, then almost fascinating: the brain, the tongue, the eyes became meat of different textures. It was hard to believe that the rubbery globes of the eyes had ever been able to receive impulses and turn them into images; still harder to believe that when they had done that, they had filled even a sheep's head with the world. To me the mechanism of sight is the principal wonder of conscious living: the mechanism which, more than any other, brings into the mind that which is outside. Sight brings in objective reality. Sight is the proof that you are as real as I am, that a pencil is as real, that a tree, a bird, a typewriter, a flower, a stone is as real; that each object is as much the centre of its universe as I am, and that conscious, human objects have each a universe as enormous as my own.

'*You are not the only pebble on the beach*' was often said to me during my childhood: words with the force of the metaphor still strong in them, since the East Anglian beaches I knew were composed almost entirely of pebbles. I used to spend hours searching among them because I collected cornelians and amber, which I kept in a jam jar, with water to make them gleam. I knew pebbles well: the different shades of grey, the almost white, the mottled, the porous, the ones with microscopic sparkles in the graining of their surfaces, the flat, the round, the potato-shaped, the totally opaque, the almost translucent. It was obvious that there was an infinite number of them, and an infinite variety, and that they were all equally real. I handled them, but more often I looked at them. It was by looking at pebbles that I began to feel their nature, and it is by looking that I feel the nature of people. 'What are you thinking?' my lover asks, and often I am not thinking, I am looking. The way the hairs of an eyebrow grow along the ridge, the slight movement under the thin skin beneath the eyes, the folding of the lips, the grain of the skin behind the ear: what I am learning from them I am not sure, but the need to study them is imperative. No doubt I should still love if I were blind, with only my reason and my hands, but could I recognize a man's separate existence in the same way?

Marcel, the diamond-polisher whose recall by Mustafa Ali released my first story, did not find objective reality a comfort. Once he leant out of a window in the Savoy Hotel, looked down on trees in which starlings were bickering their way to bed, and pavements over which people were hurrying, then slammed the window shut and exclaimed, 'I can't bear it!'

'What can't you bear?'

'The thought that I might die in the night, and next morning everything would *still be going on*. All those bastards trotting up and down the street, and those silly damned birds chirping. . . . It's horrible! Sometimes, when I'm at home, I wake in the middle of the night and start thinking about it, and then I have to telephone my sister.'

'What does she do?'

'She comes over and makes tea for me, and talks. Sometimes I keep her there all night.'

He walked up and down the room, splashing whisky out of his glass in his agitation, his mouth twitching, his eyes bilious: a sad little figure for whom the world would not come to an end.

To me, on the other hand, the knowledge that everything will *still be going on* is the answer. If I die with my wits about me, not shuffled out under drugs or reduced to incoherence by pain, I want my last thoughts to be of plants growing, children being born, people who never knew me digging their gardens or telephoning their friends. It is in the existence of other things and other people that I can feel the pulse of my own: the pulse. Something which hums and throbs in everything, and thus in me.

Reading Aldous Huxley's account of his experiments with mescalin, I caught myself thinking that this exceptionally intelligent man was naïve. The crease in his trousers, the chair and the bunch of flowers in which he discovered the vibrating truth of being: had he not known that they contained it? That every object contains it? It is true that one does not usually see it with the intensity he describes, but it is not necessary to see it in that way to know that it exists. Chemical vision-sharpeners are a luxury, not a necessity. My own (I have not seen this remarked by anyone else, but it cannot be a unique experience) comes with whatever change in glandular activity it may be that heralds menstruation, so that almost every month I have a day or two of heightened vision, a delicious spell in which to see things living.

This 'isness business'—what smartypants called it that?—is, to me, too obvious to be chic. Only the gifted mystic, in whom the necessary disciplines channel a power which already exists, is likely to get further in it by studying Buddhism: indeed, I suspect that in the East, as in the West, only the rare saints have gone beyond the man-invented paraphernalia with which the rest tag along in their wake for comfort and reassurance. It is the obviousness—the obviousness of the quiet throbbing of life in every object—which has filled for me the silence that should have been left by non-belief, and which makes me question whether I did, in fact, stop believing. Believing in what? God, I suppose, knows—if knowledge in a human sense is an attribute of whatever lies behind the throbbing, and I do not see why it should be. My senses tell me, not that 'God exists,' but that 'it is.'

The test for anyone whose balance depends on messages received through the senses will come when the senses begin to atrophy. When I can no longer see (my grandmother had not seen the stars for ten years before she died), when I can no longer hear (larks dwindled away first, she said, then all other birds), when my body, which has not only given me all my most reliable and consoling pleasures but has also helped me to go out of its limits into other people and into things, becomes no more than a painful burden—and think only of what it can do to one under the influence of something so trivial as indigestion!—what will happen then? It may turn out that the throbbing was no more than the sound of my own blood in my ears. What I hope is that even if it does I shall not be afraid, because why should that blood have throbbed so steadily, for so long, in spite of so many reasons why I need not have lived, if it were not that I too have *been,* with the same intensity as any flower or matchbox or dog or other human being: all part of something which can only be expressed in the words 'I am that which I am,' and which needs no further proof or justification?

I should like to appoint someone younger than myself to be a witness at my death: to record my success or lack of it in coming to terms with death, as I mean to do if I can, by simultaneously remembering the pulse in my self, and defeating the passion for self-preservation which makes death seem an outrage (easily said! Let the hum of an aeroplane's engine turn to a whine and my body stiffens, my stomach chills: 'Not *yet!*'). To die decently and acceptingly would be to prove the value of life, and that, in spite of limitations and inadequacy, is what I have felt inclined, still feel inclined, and have a hunch that I will always feel inclined to do.

About the Author

B ORN IN 1917 and educated at Oxford University, Diana Athill is one of the great book editors of the twentieth century. For more than five decades, she published the likes of V. S. Naipaul, John Updike, Margaret Atwood, and Jean Rhys, for whom she was a confidante and caretaker. She is the author of several memoirs, including the *New York Times* bestseller *Somewhere Towards the End* (winner of the National Book Critics Circle Award), *After a Funeral*, and *Stet*, a *New York Times* Notable Book about her fifty-year career in publishing. In 2008, the Queen of England appointed her an Officer of the British Empire. She lives in London.

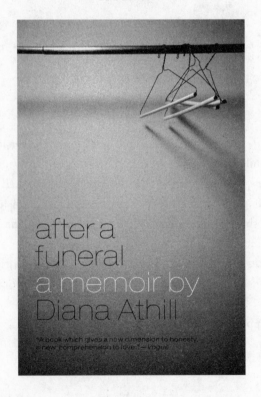

The story of how and why a talented writer came to kill himself—told with bravura, grace, and honesty— "A book which gives a new dimension to honesty, a new comprehension to love" (*Vogue*).

When Athill met the man she calls Didi, she fell in love instantly and out of love just as fast. Didi moved into her flat, they shared housework and holidays, and a life of easy intimacy seemed to beckon. But Didi's quirks, which at first appeared so charming and sweet, soon revealed a darker side—he was a gambler, a drinker, and a womanizer, impossible to live with but impossible to ignore. With painful honesty, Diana Athill explores the years she was trying to help him; a period that culminated in Didi's suicide—in her apartment—an event he described in his journals as "the one authentic act of my life."

"Anyone who believes that human relationships are important cannot fail to be moved by this book."   —*Daily Telegraph*

Somewhere Towards
the End

A Memoir

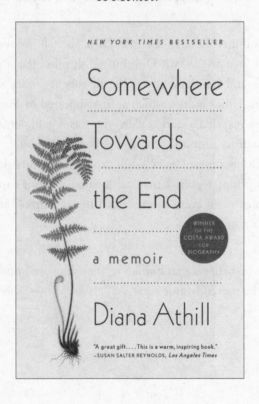

NEW YORK TIMES BESTSELLER

Somewhere
Towards
the End

a memoir

WINNER
OF THE
COSTA AWARD
FOR
BIOGRAPHY

Diana Athill

"A great gift.... This is a warm, inspiring book."
–SUSAN SALTER REYNOLDS, *Los Angeles Times*

A prize-winning, critically acclaimed memoir on life and aging—"An honest joy to read" (Alice Munro).

Hailed as "a virtuoso exercise" (*Sunday Telegraph*), this short, well-crafted book reflects candidly, sometimes with great humor, on the condition of being old. Charming readers, writers, and critics alike, the memoir won the Costa Prize and the National Book Critics Circle Award, making Athill a surprising literary star in her ninth decade.

"There is something terrifically comforting about a nonagenarian writing with clarity, wit and verve about getting old and facing death. . . . [Athill] evokes another grande dame of British letters in her uninhibited lifestyle and no-holds-barred, clarion voice: last year's Nobel Prize winner, Doris Lessing."
                        —N. Heller McAlpin, *San Francisco Chronicle*

"Unusually appealing. . . . To readers Athill delivers far more than modest pleasure: Her easy-going prose and startling honesty are riveting, for whither she has gone many of us will go as well."
                        —Michael Dirda, *Washington Post Book World*

"A great gift. . . . This is a warm, inspiring book."
                        —Susan Salter Reynolds, *Los Angeles Time*s